SUDAN

NORTH AGAINST SOUTH

SUDAN

NORTH AGAINST SOUTH

by Lawrence J. Zwier

Lerner Publications Company / Minneapolis

Website address: www.lernerbooks.com

All maps by Philip Schwartzberg, Meridian Mapping, Minneapolis.
Cover photo by Panos Pictures/Crispin Hughes
Table of contents photos (from top to bottom) by USAID/Kay Chernush;
Independent Picture Service; Independent Picture Service; Barbara Vogel.

Series Consultant: Andrew Bell-Fialkoff
Editor: Kari Cornell
Editorial Director: Mary M. Rodgers
Designer: Michael Tacheny
Photo Researcher: Adam Robbins

LIBRARY OF CONGRESS CATALOGING-IN-PUBLICATION DATA

Zwier, Lawrence J.
  Sudan: north against south / by Lawrence J. Zwier
    p. cm. — (World in conflict)
  Includes bibliographical references and index.
  Summary: Examines the history of Sudan's ethnic conflict and its
continuing effect on the people of that country.
  ISBN 0-8225-3559-9 (lib. bdg. : alk. paper)
1. Sudan—Politics and government. 2. Sudan—Ethnic relations.
3. Islam and politics—Sudan. [1. Sudan—Politics and government.
2. Sudan—ethnic relations.] I. Title. II. Series.

DT155.6.Z94   1999
320.9624—dc21   97-46180

Manufactured in the United States of America
1 2 3 4 5 6 – JR – 04 03 02 01 00 99

CONTENTS

ABOUT THIS SERIES

Government firepower kills 25 protesters . . . . Thousands of refugees flee the country . . . . Rebels attack capital . . . . Racism and rage flare . . . . Fighting breaks out . . . . Peace talks stall . . . . Bombing toll rises to 52 . . . . Slaughter has cost up to 50,000 lives.

Conflicts between people occur across the globe, and we hear about some of the more spectacular and horrific episodes in the news. But since most fighting doesn't directly affect us, we often choose to ignore it. And even if we do take the time to learn about these conflicts—from newspapers, magazines, television news, or radio—we're often left with just a snapshot of the conflict instead of the whole reel of film.

Most news accounts don't tell you the whole story about a conflict, focusing instead on the attention-grabbing events that make the headlines. In addition, news sources may have a preconceived idea about who is right and who is wrong in a conflict. The stories that result often portray one side as the "bad guys" and the other as the "good guys."

The *World in Conflict* series approaches each conflict with the idea that wars and political disputes aren't simply about bullies and victims. Conflicts are complex problems that can often be traced back hundreds of years. The people fighting one another have complicated reasons for doing so. Fighting erupts between groups divided by ethnicity, religion, and nationalism. These groups fight over power, money, territory, control. Sometimes people who just want to go about their own business get caught up in a conflict just because they're there.

These books examine major conflicts around the world, some of which are very bloody and others that haven't involved a lot of violence. They portray the people involved in and affected by conflicts. They describe how each conflict got started, how it developed, and where it stands. The books also outline some of the ways people have tried to end the conflicts. By reading the stories behind the headlines, you will learn some reasons why people hate and fight one another and, in addition, why some people struggle so hard to end conflicts.

WORDS YOU NEED TO KNOW

autonomous: an area or territory that is part of a larger political unit but has self-governing powers.

Communist: A person who supports Communism—an economic system in which government owns the means of producing goods in factories and of growing food.

condominium: A government operating under joint rule by two or more nations.

displaced: People who have been forced to flee from their homeland due to famine or civil war.

dissident: A person who disagrees with an established religious or political system, organization, or belief.

ethnic group: A permanent group of people bonded together by a combination of cultural markers, which may include—but are not limited to—race, nationality, tribe, religion, language, customs, and historical origins.

fundamentalist: A person or group of people who stress strict and literal adherance to a set of basic principles. In Sudan, fundamentalist groups advocate the rigid enforcement of sharia.

infrastructure: The system of roads, schools, and other resources used by the public and maintained by the government of the country, state, or region.

Islamist: A person who holds strongly to the faith, doctrine, or cause of Islam.

media: A system of communication, information, or entertainment, such as newspapers, magazines, books, radio, or television. Media can also include the reporters or correspondents who gather the information that appears in newspapers, magazines, or on television.

nationalism: A feeling of loyalty or patriotism toward one's nation, with a primary emphasis on the promotion of a national culture and national interests.

right-wing: Political parties or other organizations whose members oppose change in the established system or government and who favor traditional attitudes.

secession: To formally withdraw membership from a political unit, such as a nation, or from an organization, such as the United Nations. The seceding group usually desires increased independence or autonomy.

sharia: A set of strict Islamic laws introduced into Sudan in 1983 by President Nimeiri.

FOREWORD

by Andrew Bell-Fialkoff

Conflicts between various groups are as old as time. Peoples and tribes around the world have fought one another for thousands of years. In fact our history is in great part a succession of wars—between the Greeks and the Persians, the English and the French, the Russians and the Poles, and many others. Not only do states or ethnic groups fight one another, so do followers of different religions—Catholics and Protestants in Northern Ireland, Christians and Muslims in Bosnia, and Buddhists and Hindus in Sri Lanka. Often ethnicity, language, and religion—some of the main distinguishing elements of culture—reinforce one another in characterizing a particular group. For instance, the vast majority of Greeks are Orthodox Christian and speak Greek; most Italians are Roman Catholic and speak Italian. Elsewhere, one cultural aspect predominates. Serbs and Croats speak dialects of the same language but remain separate from one another because most Croats are Catholics and most Serbs are Orthodox Christians. To those two groups, religion is more important than language in defining culture.

We have witnessed an increasing number of conflicts in modern times—why? Three reasons stand out. One is that large empires—such as Austria-Hungary, Ottoman Turkey, several colonial empires with vast holdings in Asia, Africa, and America, and, most recently, the Soviet Union—have collapsed. A look at world maps from 1900, 1950, and 1998 reveals an ever-increasing number of small and medium-sized states. While empires existed, their rulers suppressed many ethnic and religious conflicts. Empires imposed order, and local resentments were mostly directed at the central authority. Inside the borders of empires, populations were multiethnic and often highly mixed. When the empires fell apart, world leaders found it impossible to establish political frontiers that coincided with ethnic boundaries. Different groups often claimed territories inhabited by others. The nations created on the lands of a toppled empire were saddled with acute border and ethnic problems from their very beginnings.

The second reason for more conflicts in modern times stems from the twin ideals of freedom and equality. In the United States, we usually think of freedom as "individual freedom." If we all have equal rights, we are free. But if you are a member of a minority group and feel that you are being discriminated against, your group's rights and freedoms are also important to you. In fact, if you don't have your "group freedom," you don't have full individual freedom either.

After World War I (1914–1918), the allied western nations, under the guidance of U.S. president Woodrow Wilson, tried to satisfy group rights by promoting minority rights. The spread of frantic nationalism in the 1930s, especially among disaffected ethnic minorities, and the catastrophe of World War II (1939–1945) led to a fundamental

SUDAN *North against South*

reassessment of the Wilsonian philosophy. After 1945 group rights were downplayed on the assumption that guaranteeing individual rights would be sufficient. In later decades, the collapse of multiethnic nations like Czechoslovakia, Yugoslavia, and the Soviet Union—coupled with the spread of nationalism in those regions—came as a shock to world leaders. People want democracy and individual rights, but they want their group rights, too. In practice, this means more conflicts and a cycle of secession, as minority ethnic groups seek their own sovereignty and independence.

The fires of conflict are often further stoked by the media, which lavishes glory and attention on independence movements. To fight for freedom is an honor. For every Palestinian who has killed an Israeli, there are hundreds of Kashmiris, Tamils, and Bosnians eager to shoot at their enemies. Newspapers, television and radio news broadcasts, and other media play a vital part in fomenting that sense of honor. They magnify each crisis, glorify rebellion, and help to feed the fire of conflict.

The third factor behind increasing conflict in the world is the social and geographic mobility that modern society enjoys. We can move anywhere we want and can aspire—or so we believe—to be anything we wish. Every day the television tantalizingly dangles the prizes that life can offer. We all want our share. But increased mobility and ambition also mean increased competition, which leads to antagonism. Antagonism often fastens itself to ethnic, racial, or religious differences. If you are an inner-city African American and your local grocer happens to be Korean American, you may see that individual as different from yourself—an intruder—rather than as a person, a neighbor, or a grocer. This same feeling of "us" versus "them" has been part of many an ethnic conflict around the world.

Many conflicts have been contained—even solved—by wise, responsible leadership. But unfortunately, many politicians use citizens' discontent for their own ends. They incite hatred, manipulate voters, and mobilize people against their neighbors. The worst things happen when neighbor turns against neighbor. In Bosnia, in Rwanda, in Lebanon, and in countless other places, people who had lived and worked together and had even intermarried went on a rampage, killing, raping, and robbing one another with gusto. If the appalling carnage teaches us anything, it is that we should stop seeing one another as hostile competitors and enemies and accept one another as people. Most importantly, we should learn to understand why conflicts happen and how they can be prevented. That is why *World in Conflict* is so important—the books in this series will help you understand the history and inner dynamics of some of the most persistent conflicts of modern times. And understanding is the first step to prevention. ⊕

INTRODUCTION

The Republic of Sudan is the largest country in Africa. With an area of 967,500 square miles, the nation is larger than Texas and Alaska combined. Located in the northeastern part of the continent, Sudan is bounded on the north by Egypt and on the east by the Red Sea, Eritrea, and Ethiopia. Kenya, Uganda, and the Democratic Republic of Congo (DRC, formerly Zaire) are Sudan's southern neighbors. The Central African Republic, Chad, and Libya lie to the west.

NORTH AND SOUTH

The most important geographical division within Sudan is an informal distinction between the north and the south. Roughly speaking, the south comprises the area south of the Bahr al-Ghazal (river) and the Sobat River. The difference between the two areas goes beyond climate or location to basic culture.

The north is predominantly Arabic-speaking, follows the faith of Islam, and feels culturally tied to North Africa. In the south, Arab influence is far weaker. Local languages and English prevail, and most people are Christians or adherents of local religions. Southerners share a general sense of cultural kinship with various parts of equatorial Africa (countries that border the equator).

Although informal, this north-south division is very real—real enough to fuel long periods of civil war since 1956, when Sudan gained independence from Great Britain and Egypt. The present conflict began in 1983 and has resulted in the deaths of as many as 1 million people through fighting or famine. Estimates have put the number of people **displaced** between 1.5 and 3.5 million.

Fighting flared between the northern-based government forces and the southern rebel groups when the government divided the south into three administrative units. The division diluted the power of the Dinka, the region's largest **ethnic group,** and southern

Facing page: *When European countries drew Sudan's borders long ago, they neglected to consider the various ethnic groups whose homelands extended into Sudan from neighboring countries. At two points, Sudan's borders remain under dispute. In the south, Kenya claims and occupies a small region that, according to internationally recognized boundaries, is actually part of Sudan. In the north, Egypt claims—and has occasionally occupied—a small Sudanese region known as the Hala'ib Triangle along the Red Sea coast.*

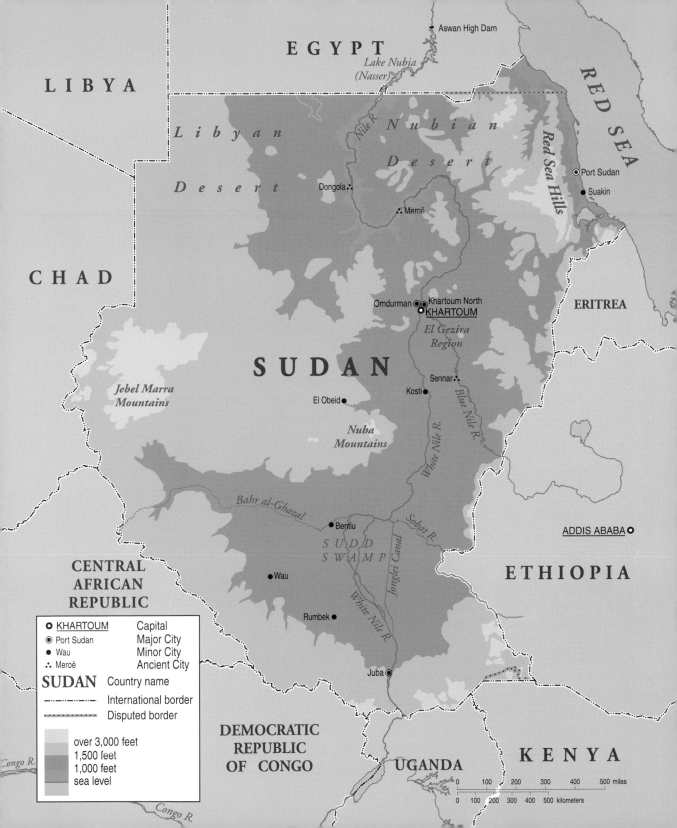

Much of the land in northern Sudan is dry and barren. Farmers use regions that are too far from the Nile River for grazing.

© USAID

rebel groups responded by taking up arms. The government's next move, to impose a set of strict Islamic laws, called **sharia,** added fuel to the fire.

Depending on how it's interpreted, sharia may restrict the public activities of women and forbid some activities that non-Muslims consider innocent and harmless. Many southerners are adamantly opposed to sharia. They resent the government's insistence that it's the law, even for people who don't follow Islam. These southerners fear that the national government, dominated by northerners, will force the Arabic language and the Islamic religion on the south. Southerners worry that the north will use the south's resources to benefit northerners.

THE LAND

From north to south, Sudan's landscape changes dramatically. Much of the northern third of Sudan is a desert that is part of Africa's huge Sahara region. Farther south, the desert gives way to sparsely vegetated dunes, then to irrigated clay plains, semi-arid grassland, and open woodlands dotted with acacia and thorn trees. In the far south, especially near the border with the DRC, the land is well watered, receiving as much as 47 inches of rain per year. This amount is enough to sustain thick forests and substantial agricultural crops.

One district in south central Sudan, the Sudd, is the world's largest swamp. This reedy region is interlaced with rivulets that are part of the Nile River system. An area just north of the Sudd, on the border between the central province of Kordofan and Bahr al-Ghazal, a province in the southwest, has some oil reserves.

The Nile—at 4,145 miles, the longest river in the

world—flows from south to north through Sudan and shapes the country's patterns of agriculture and settlement. In Sudan, there are actually two Niles. The shorter Blue Nile travels north from Ethiopia in the east. The longer White Nile takes a more westerly course, running from Uganda into southern Sudan.

The two Niles meet at Sudan's capital, Khartoum, and continue northward, making several great bends on the way to the Egyptian border and the Mediterranean Sea. Four cataracts—rapids where the river is impassable to most boats—mark the river's course through northern Sudan. Near the border with

Egypt, the Nile flows into Lake Nubia, the Sudanese name for the southern end of Lake Nasser, a reservoir formed by Egypt's Aswan High Dam.

The importance of the Nile to the Sudanese, especially to northerners, is immeasurable. Water from the river enables farmers to grow crops in the deserts of the region. From an airplane, the Nile of the north runs through a thin ribbon of green never more than about a mile and a quarter wide. The Nile supplies irrigation water for huge agricultural projects in east central Sudan.

THE PEOPLE
Like many other African countries, Sudan had its

Two rivers, the Bahr al-Ghazal and the White Nile, water the swampy Sudd region in the south. During the rainy season, the Nile floods and vegetation flourishes.

© D.H. Condit

boundaries drawn by foreign colonial authorities. As a result, within the country's borders live many different ethnic groups. Although no one is really sure, estimates suggest that about 572 different peoples make their homes in Sudan.

Sudanese ethnic groups are usually first characterized as either Muslim (followers of Islam) or non-Muslim. Approximately 66 percent of the population is Muslim. Most Muslims, who have long been politically dominant, live in the northern three-fourths of the country. The non-Muslims are more likely to live in the south. Five percent of the Sudanese are Christian, and about 25 percent follow local religions.

Muslims encompass a wide range of Sudan's ethnic groups, including the Arabs, the Nubians of the northern Nile Valley, the Fur of the Jebel Marra to the west, and the Beja of the Red Sea Hills to the east. Of these groups, the Arabs are by far the largest, making up about 40 percent of the entire population of the country. It is difficult to say what Arab means anywhere, but in Sudan the definition is

Language

Arabic, Sudan's official language, is used in government and the national media. The language exists in several forms, the most widespread of which is Modern Standard Arabic, an international language of everyday affairs. In reality, Sudan has developed several of its own local dialects of standard Arabic that outsiders cannot always understand.

Life is much easier for Sudanese who can speak Arabic, but many citizens, especially in the south, see the language as a politically distasteful imposition. The number of different languages spoken by the Sudanese is probably close to 400, but many tongues appear among only a few hundred people who live in remote regions. For this reason, English is widely employed in the south as a contact language for people who speak different local languages.

Sudanese law allows elementary or middle schools to teach in English and many in the south prefer English because their only other legal choice is Arabic. Even in the north, despite the dominance of Arabic, English is a commonly spoken second or third language and is a required subject in school.

These Muslim girls attend an all-girl Islamic school in Khartoum, the Sudanese capital, where lessons are taught in Arabic.

particularly troublesome. Census takers usually include as an Arab anyone who identifies himself or herself as such. But this does not necessarily mean that every Arab is a native speaker of Arabic whose ancestors are from the Arabian Peninsula. Many of the self-identified Arabs in Sudan have at least partial black African ancestry.

The non-Muslims are almost all black Africans. Most of them live in the south, but some have moved to the Three Towns of the north (Khartoum, Omdurman, and Khartoum North) or to other big towns such as Kosti, El Obeid, and Port Sudan. Many speak English in addition to their own local language. The southern Sudanese are often classified into large language-culture groups. One such group, the Nilotics, includes Sudan's two largest southern ethnic groups, the Dinka and the Nuer. The Dinka and Nuer languages are very different but are historically related to one another. Nilotic

Above: *This boy from the Dinka ethnic group is dressed in modern clothes but carries the spear and wears the traditional jewelry of his ancestors.* Right: *People from the Azande ethnic group shop at an outdoor market in southern Sudan.*

Of Sudan's approximately 25 million people, fewer than 20 percent live in cities or towns. Most are small-scale farmers or herders, like these Nuer cattle herders from southern Sudan, who live in villages near their fields or grazing lands. More than 10 percent of the Sudanese are nomads—people who roam with their flocks from pasture to pasture and have no fixed residence.

groups also share certain cultural traits. For example, cattle raising is very important in Nilotic cultures, and social standing can depend upon the number of cattle a person owns. Another Nilotic characteristic is a tradition of decentralized government, in which villages or even extended families govern their own affairs instead of being under a strong king or central government.

The south holds many other ethnic groups—the Azande, the Shilluk, and more. But the south is not the only part of Sudan where non-Muslim groups live. The Murle and Didinga peoples, for example, make their homes near the Ethiopian border. A significant cluster of traditionally non-Muslim groups, collectively called the Nuba people, live in the Nuba Mountains of central Sudan.

They have cultural ties to peoples in Chad and in countries west of Sudan.

THE FRACTIOUS FACTIONS

The unrest in Sudan is complicated, involving many different rebel groups and resistance organizations. Each represents seemingly irreconcilable currents within Sudanese society—the Muslim and the non-Muslim, the secular and the religious, those who want Sudan to stay united and those who want it to split apart.

The strongest, best-organized resistance force is the Sudan People's Liberation Army (SPLA), which is

Most southern Sudanese are likely to feel a closer link with their relatives in Chad, Ethiopia, or the DRC than with their near neighbors in Sudan.

under the command of Colonel John Garang. The SPLA's leadership and fighting force are mostly Dinka, including Christians and followers of traditional religions. They and other rebel groups survive by getting support from civilians in the south. The rebels also enjoy backing from governments and factions in neighboring Ethiopia, Eritrea, and Uganda—countries whose leaders fear a Sudan ruled by a unified Islamic regime.

Among southern rebels, disagreement is widespread, largely over whether the south should stay within Sudan or become an independent nation. Garang's branch of the SPLA insists that Sudan should remain united but under a secular regime. Other rebel groups, notably the mostly Nuer South Sudan Independence Movement (SSIM), want full independence for the south.

Ethnic distrust also fuels discord among the southern rebels. Some non-Dinkas are suspicious that, if the SPLA were to take control, insensitive rule by Dinkas would simply replace insensitive rule by northern Arabs.

The Khartoum government insists on its right to enforce peace within Sudan's borders. It points out that order is necessary for Sudan to emerge from poverty. Repeated attempts to negotiate a settlement with the rebels have failed, Khartoum says, so military action is unavoidable.

Similarly, many see the government's imposition of sharia on non-Muslims as harsh. But influential people in the Khartoum government feel morally bound, according to their interpretation of Islam, to reform all of Sudanese society according to Islamic principles. Called **Islamists,** these people are the leading force in national Sudanese politics.

The National Islamic Front (NIF), whose spiritual leader is Hassan al-Turabi, holds most of the power in the Sudanese government. The NIF is a **fundamentalist** Islamic party dedicated to the enforcement of sharia throughout the country.

Other key political parties have been declared illegal and do not support government policies. The Democratic Unionist Party (DUP), for example, is pro-Egyptian and is strongly opposed to a strict application of Islamic law. The Umma Party is a **right-wing,** Muslim political group that wins most of its support from the Ansar Muslim sect of the provinces of Darfur and Kordofan. The NIF, DUP, Umma Party and other associations, each with its own interpretation of correct Islamic practice, jockey for power over Sudan. Those

Rebel-held Areas

In the late 1990s, the areas under rebel control included the countryside and small villages in southern Sudan. The SPLA also controlled a few medium-sized towns, including Rumbek. But for the most part, the government held the cities and larger towns, notably Juba, Wau, and Malakal. This situation has created a classic guerrilla-war pattern in the south. The SPLA strikes government positions sporadically, ambushing government patrols and trying to drive government soldiers from garrison towns. In 1997 the SPLA and some allied rebel groups also gained control of a few towns in the extreme east along the borders with Ethiopia and Eritrea.

who come up short—including former prime minister Sadiq al-Mahdi, a member of the Umma Party, and former president Colonel Jaafar Mohammed Nimeiri—are likely to find themselves in jail or in exile. Factions in the military or among intellectuals who think they can do better than the current leaders have frequently attempted to overthrow the government.

THE ECONOMY

Farming and herding are the most important economic activities in Sudan—even in areas that, to an outsider, may seem too dry. About two-thirds of all the workers in Sudan have occupations related to agriculture. Besides growing vegetables and fruit for local consumption, Sudanese farmers raise cotton, peanuts, sorghum (a grain that grows in tropical climates), and some wheat for export. Another important export is gum arabic, a component in glues, candies, and soft drinks. Gum arabic comes from the sap of acacia trees that grow naturally in many parts of central Sudan. Nomads herd camels, cattle, goats, and sheep extensively, too. Most of the meat, wool, and dairy products are for local use.

Since the mid-1980s, below-average rainfall has caused severe droughts throughout Sudan. Aside from destroying crops, the drought has disrupted the labor supply by forcing people to move to ur-

ban areas where they can get food. Rebel and government troops have snatched up the few plants that have managed to take root in the parched soil, leaving civilians to starve. To compound matters, famines in neighboring countries like Eritrea, Ethiopia, Chad, and Uganda have driven refugees into Sudan, causing further strain on the crippled Sudanese economy.

Other factors also play into Sudan's economic challenges. Sudan's huge size makes governing difficult. Khartoum, the seat of government, is at least 600 miles away from 80 percent of the nation. Only about 40 percent of Sudanese men—and only 11 percent of the women—can read. The average male lives to the age

Fertile Land in the North

El Gezira (meaning "island" in Arabic) is a wedge of land southeast of Khartoum that is bordered on the northeast by the Blue Nile and on the west by the White Nile. This area is part of a huge clay plain that stretches along Sudan's boundary with Ethiopia. Despite looking like cracked wasteland during dry times, El Gezira is very fertile. When irrigated with water from both of the Niles, the land can support vast fields of cotton, vegetables, and grain. It's ironic that, Sudan, which is periodically wracked by famine, has a lot of cultivated land and is often portrayed as a potential breadbasket for the Arab world. So far, Sudan has not succeeded in being a breadbasket for itself.

of 51, and the average woman to about 54. Nearly 10 percent of the babies born in Sudan die as infants. Clean drinking water is often hard to find, and water-borne diseases like cholera are common.

Costs, especially for food, have been rising, but incomes have not. Fewer Sudanese can afford to eat a balanced diet. Food riots are common—even though the police deal brutally with demonstrators. Various governments since the 1970s have been tragically ineffective in dealing with basic issues of survival. Unrest erupts in nearly every segment of the population, not just among the non-Muslims in the south.

And finally there is the civil war. Primarily a clash of cul-

tures—one with strong religious overtones—the issue of control is also key. The government has always been in the hands of Arabic-speaking Muslims, and various non-Muslim peoples throughout the country resent the authority these rulers want to exert. The south maintains a centuries-old resentment of northern invaders.

Amid all of this instability, Sudan struggles to stay together as a state. But whether it should is another question. Can so large a state, encompassing so many groups within not-very-rational colonial borders, survive? There has been an independent Sudan for more than 40 years. Many observers believe it cannot last. ⊕

Facing page: *Dams like this one on the Nile in northern Sudan provide farmers with water for their crops.*

MAJOR PLAYERS IN THE CONFLICT

General Omar Hassan al-Bashir

Riek Machar

SSIM Emblem

al-Bashir, General Omar Hassan Leader of Sudan since 1989, when he seized power through a military coup.

Garang, Colonel John Leader of the Sudan People's Liberation Army (SPLA) since 1982.

Machar, Riek Leader of the South Sudanese Independence Movement (SSIM) and the Southern Coordination Council.

National Democratic Alliance (NDA) A Cairo-based political organization formed in the mid-1990s when disaffected northerners joined forces with the South Sudanese Independence Movement.

National Islamic Front (NIF) A fundamentalist Sudanese Islamic party that favors the enforcement of sharia laws.

South Sudanese Independence Movement (SSIM) Once part of the Sudan People's Liberation Army, this mostly Nuer rebel faction broke away in 1991 when leaders of the two groups disagreed about the best way to resolve Sudan's conflict. The SSIM favors an independent south.

Southern Coordination Council Created when the NIF and the SSIM signed a peace agreement in April 1997, the purpose of this 25-member council is to facilitate communication between the southern provinces.

Sudan People's Liberation Army (SPLA) A rebel group opposed to Islamic rule that has fought a civil war against the Sudanese government since 1984. The SPLA draws most of its support from the Dinka ethnic group. Because the SPLA favors a unified Sudan, free from Islamic rule, the group does not support the April 1997 peace agreement reached between the SSIM and the NIF.

SPLA Emblem

al-Turabi, Hassan Leader of the National Islamic Front based in Khartoum, al-Turabi has a great deal of influence on the military regime of General Omar Hassan al-Bashir. Al-Turabi is the main force behind the push to impose sharia throughout Sudan.

Reuters/Corinne Dufka/Archive Photos

Hassan al-Turabi

Umma Party (UP) This group was the largest political party in Sudan during the most recent period of parliamentary democracy. Most of its supporters live in the rural areas of western Darfur province and Kordofan province. Although the Umma Party is an Islamic political party whose members favor the enforcement of sharia, followers would rather seek an end to the civil war than impose strict Islamic law on southerners. The UP is a member of the NDA.

UP Emblem

CHAPTER 1

THE RECENT CONFLICT AND ITS EFFECTS

Reports coming out of Sudan these days echo news from 1983. Battles between the government troops and the SPLA go on, although neither side seems to gain much ground. In late January 1998, the rebels appeared to be making progress. But after attacking and holding three towns in southwestern Sudan, the government forces soon pushed back the rebels into the surrounding countryside. Government troops continue to control all major towns and cities, while the rebels hold the rural areas. Clashes with rebel forces have cost an impoverished nation at least $1 million each day.

Much of the fighting remains in the south, but unrest near the Eritrean border has been increasing. The government, eager to squelch any sense that the rebellion is spreading, claimed that the eastern fighting did not

© Agence France Presse/ Corbis-Bettmann

A Sudan People's Liberation Army (SPLA) soldier examines the damage after his army conquered Yei, a town just southwest of Juba, the south's largest and most important city.

Hungry Sudanese wait at a landing strip for relief food to be unloaded from the airplanes that the government has allowed to land.

involve Sudanese rebels, only commandos from Eritrea.

STILL FIGHTING FAMINE

Aid agencies are estimating that about 700,000 people are still in danger of starving in southern Sudan. Getting supplies and food to hungry Sudanese has never been easy. In the past, the government has imposed bans on aircraft carrying relief sup-plies into southern provinces. Although such bans were lifted in February 1998, all flights must still be cleared with Khartoum at least one month in advance.

Meanwhile, conditions in the Bahr al-Ghazal, home to many Dinka people, are the worst they've been since 1983. People have resorted to scrounging for seeds in dry riverbeds or even in ant nests. The number of malnourished children is also on the rise.

People have resorted to scrounging for seeds in dry riverbeds or even in ant nests.

A DISPLACED PEOPLE

Unlike the famine in Ethiopia, Sudan's most recent famine hasn't resulted from drought alone. It's a disaster caused by people. Since January 1998, renewed artillery attacks between government troops and SPLA forces have pushed 24,000 people from villages in eastern Sudan, leaving them unable to grow crops or to raise cattle to sustain themselves. Sudan-based correspondents for the British Broadcasting Corporation (BBC) reported that fighting had rendered more than 100,000 Sudanese homeless in January and February of 1998 alone. Since 1983 approximately three million Sudanese, more than 10 percent of the nation's population, have fled their homes to escape the violence.

Some of these displaced people live in refugee camps in Sudan or in neighboring countries. Although the camps provide basic food and shelter, residents have little opportunity to improve their living conditions. Other displaced Sudanese make their homes in slums on the outskirts of Khartoum or other cities. These slums are full

Two of an estimated 240,000 displaced Beja people wait for relief food in a refugee camp near the Red Sea coastal city of Suakin. The civil war has forced thousands of southerners to leave their homes.

of disease, and crime is common. Resources are stretched very thin, and there's little extra food or money to go around.

A Sudanese refugee may have fled home for several reasons. Home may no longer exist, having been burned down or destroyed by

A villager sifts through her belongings after bombing raids by government troops destroyed her home in southern Sudan.

artillery shells in a battle between the government and one of the rebel groups. Even if the walls of a refugee's house are still standing, they may be riddled with bullet holes or stained with blood. Flight to escape unbearable memories is not unusual in Sudan. Many Sudanese refugees have survived attacks in which rebels or government troops killed entire villages to punish inhabitants for supposedly helping the wrong side. They can no longer stand the strain of living in a contested area, where every day holds the threat of an attack.

Sudan's refugee problem has international aspects, too. Many people displaced by the fighting have fled to the Three Towns region, swelling populations there beyond the area's ability to cope. One of General Omar Hassan al-Bashir's earliest acts as ruler was to return some 600,000 southern refugees to the south. Unwelcome in their own capital, many Sudanese refugees have fled to neighboring countries like Uganda or Ethiopia. They live in camps administered by the United Nations High Commissioner for Refugees (UNHCR).

And even as people have fled Sudan for elsewhere, Sudan continues to harbor nearly 400,000 foreign refugees from turmoil in Rwanda, Ethiopia, Eritrea, the DRC, and other countries. The UNHCR is slowly sending some back to their homelands.

MILITARY SERVITUDE
Many Sudanese have fled to avoid being forced by either the government or the rebels to serve in an army. Human-rights groups have accused the SPLA of seizing children as young as 12 for military service. The rebels deny forcing anyone under 18 to join their troops. Reports by the UN and by the U.S. State Department have repeatedly charged the Khartoum government with capturing unwilling civilians for military service and other

tasks. According to a March 1998 *New York Times* article, the government has forced young male students in Khartoum into military service as soon as they graduate from high school. The military often neglects to inform the families about these new recruits.

Wealthy families have sent their teenage sons abroad on tourist visas to keep them out of the army. Leaving isn't a wise option for those who do end up serving in the military. On April 2, 1998, for example, Sudanese soldiers killed 74 students who were trying to escape. More than 55 recruits drowned when their getaway boat capsized on the Blue Nile. Autopsies indicated that some of the dead also suffered from bullet wounds. Of all the students killed, the government returned only 12 to their families for burial. They buried the rest in mass graves four days after the incident had occurred.

Both sides have forced boys as young as 12 years old to join the fight. This young southerner is under the command of John Garang's faction of the SPLA.

No News

Although civil war and famine have plagued Sudan since 1983, news of the country's desperate situation wasn't widespread until 1988, when severe floods wiped out what few crops remained. News crews from around the world had been busy covering famines in nearby Somalia and Ethiopia, but they had virtually ignored similar conditions in Sudan.

For many years, the Sudanese government had banned reporters and other foreigners from the southern provinces, where war and famine had done the most damage. When journalists were allowed into the country, many were not willing to submit themselves to the risks involved in reporting from southern Sudan. Limited roads hamper travel through the harsh terrain. Those who found their way into the remote war zones had to deal with bombings, land mines, and sweltering heat.

Forced service in Sudan goes all the way to outright slavery. According to the U.S. State Department, two American journalists were able to buy two children in a Sudanese market while they were investigating Sudan's slave trade. These reports support numerous UN reports of a thriving trade of black Africans from southern Sudan being sold to northern Sudanese buyers.

DAILY LIFE

Freedom of many kinds is hard to come by in Sudan. The Sudanese government maintains tight control over all forms of the **media.** Officials frequently fire or jail teachers, clerics, and others who publicly say what the government doesn't want its citizens to hear. Public frustration with the regime periodically leads to urban riots. The government responds to such outbreaks quickly with military force. Fundamentalist Islamic officials further limit public speech and behavior through a strict interpretation of Islamic law. No public concerts are held in Sudan, for example, and movie theaters and dance clubs are illegal. Sudan's religious authorities say these activities are contrary to the teachings of Islam.

The chaos in the country affects the lives of ordinary Sudanese. Their villages have become battlefields. Raiding militias have split up families. Travel is hazardous, especially in the south, with large areas of the country virtually impassable because of the risk from bandits, kidnappers, and land mines.

Air travel is either dangerous or impossible. In 1986, rebels shot down a commercial flight that Sudan Airways, the national airline, operated. All 60 Sudanese civilians on board died in the crash. Since then, most airlines have canceled service to Sudan. This event is just a symptom of a nation whose conflict has deep historical roots. ⊕

Christian Solidarity International (CSI) reports that a child slave in Sudan sells for about US$300. The price is higher if the buyer is a foreigner.

CHAPTER 2

THE CONFLICT'S ROOTS

Northern Sudan's early history is fairly well documented. Much less is known about the south. The north had dealings with cultures that kept written records—the Egyptians, the Persians, the Greeks, and the Romans.

By contrast, it is not even possible to say which of the present-day southern peoples had ancestors living in Sudan 1,500 or 2,000 years ago. Not until Islam arrived and established itself firmly in Sudan did records of the southern peoples begin to surface.

In the north, the ancient civilization of the Nile Valley flourished not only in Egypt but also in Sudan, especially after 2000 B.C., when trade links between the two regions had developed. The Nile Valley of northern Sudan, often called Nubia, sometimes fell under the control of the Egyptians. But when the Egyptian pharaohs (rulers) were weak, the Nubian cities were self-ruling, at least until about 1500 B.C. At that point, the Egyptian kingdom grew immensely powerful, and

Jenny Pate/The Hutchison Library

The El Nuri Pyramids in northern Sudan are evidence of Egyptian influence in early Sudanese society.

Drawings that depict everyday life in early Egypt can be found inside the pyramids in northern Sudan.

THE COMING OF ISLAM

Islam, the religion that the prophet Muhammed had established on the Arabian Peninsula in around A.D. 630, aimed at expanding the number of believers and land area of its followers. Within only a few years of Muhammed's death in 632, military conquests had brought Islam quickly westward into Egypt. Because Egypt strongly influenced northern Sudanese culture, Islam eventually made its way to Sudan. The faith didn't extend far into northern Sudan until many centuries later, however, when the religion spread peacefully, not by war. At first the Nubians strongly resisted Islam. So the Muslims who ruled Egypt arranged a series of treaties, called *baqt*, whereby Nubians exchanged slaves for Egyptian goods. This agreement allowed Muslim armies, traders, and religious leaders to enter Nubia,

Nubia became an extension of the Egyptian Empire. The Egyptians called northern Sudan the province of Kush. The people of Kush worshiped Egyptian gods and adopted Egyptian ways of burying the dead, of farming the Nile's floodplain, and of keeping calendars.

In A.D. 350, the kingdom of Aksum in Ethiopia conquered and ransacked Meroë, an ancient Nubian city north of Khartoum. Aksum was Christian, and its conquest of Meroë spread Christianity throughout the northern and eastern parts of present-day Sudan. No central authority enforced this religion. Instead, various small states in the region operated independently of one another, some of them worshiping traditional Egyptian gods, others following Christianity, still others adhering to local religions.

especially the city-state of Dongola on the Nile. The slow immigration of Muslims led to the establishment of a Muslim power base.

By 1315 Islam had taken hold in Dongola and was spreading across the region. By about 1500, it had displaced Christianity in all of the northern kingdoms and city-states of Sudan. A kingdom called Soba near the Blue Nile was the last Christian stronghold to fall. A people called the Funj, who were probably descended from the Nubians and from peoples of the Ethiopian borderlands, had established a powerful sultanate (kingdom ruled by a sultan) at a town called Sennar along the Blue Nile. They were not Arabs, and, at first, they were not Muslims either, but they did eventually convert to Islam. Although their lands didn't stretch much beyond what would become east central Sudan, the Funj kept this region solidly Muslim, despite the power of Christian Ethiopia to the east.

Another powerful Muslim sultanate arose in western Sudan. The Fur people of Jebel Marra became the preeminent group of the region, herding camels and monitoring commerce from the western Sahara. Muslim but not Arab, the Fur established a strong central government based at the city of Al Fashir. From there they controlled much of west cen-

Understanding Islam

To concentrate on Islamic military or political history risks forgetting that Islam is, at its heart, a religious faith. The majority of Muslims in Sudan view it as a way to worship God and as a code of conduct, not as a political or military cause.

Hundreds of millions of people worldwide—including more than 15 million Sudanese—follow Islam. Many different interpretations and strains of belief exist among Muslims, but all Muslims agree on five basic principles.

Most important among them, Muslims believe that there is only one god (Allah), who created all things and to whom all humans must submit. *Islam,* in fact, is a classical Arabic word meaning "submission" and *Muslim* means "one who submits." After death Muslims hope to reach paradise, a state of peace and contentment, possible only if they have lived good lives. Allah is merciful, but angels keep track of a person's good and bad deeds. Everyone will be judged after death.

Islam expects its followers not to kill, steal, cause injury to others, or have intimate relations outside of marriage. Muslims are also expected to pray five times a day according to a set ritual that includes washing, bowing, and acknowledging God's greatness. During the Muslim month of Ramadan, Muslims must fast from dawn until dusk. And at least once during their lives, Muslims are required to make a pilgrimage (the Hajj) to the holy city of Mecca in Saudi Arabia. Since the Hajj can be expensive and physically challenging, only healthy Muslims who can afford to are expected to make the trip.

Islam holds that God has spoken to humans through several prophets, including some who also appear in Judaism or Christianity, such as Abraham and Moses. The last of the prophets, and the one most honored by Muslims, is Muhammed.

In the 1800s, most of the southern peoples suffered from slave raids. The largest groups—including the Dinka and the Nuer—fought against the slavers. Smaller groups, however, were severely depopulated, and some peoples were wiped out altogether. This period of full-scale slaving established a pattern. Northern outsiders would arrive to capture slaves, driving southerners from their homes and families.

tral Sudan, sometimes as far south as the Bahr al-Ghazal and as far east as the White Nile. But alongside the Fur Sultanate, other smaller political groupings existed.

SOUTHERN SETTLEMENT

Although Islam was firmly established in northern and western Sudan, Arabs didn't inhabit these areas. They were probably a minor, although influential, part of the Sudanese population at this time. Arab traders and Christian missionaries occasionally traveled far enough south on the Nile to reach southern Sudan, but most found the swamps so formidable that the area was named al-Sudd, Arabic for "the obstruction." Others made their way into the region from the Indian Ocean ports of Mombasa and Zanzibar in eastern Africa. Still others entered via the Saharan caravan routes. Sometimes the traders were interested in gum arabic or ivory. But many traders came

Courtesy of Kenneth J. Perkins

Ancient Sudanese Culture

The largest archaeological site in Sudan is at Meroë, on the east bank of the Nile south of Atbara. It dates from about 2000 years ago, long after the Egyptian empire had crumbled under successive invasions by the Persians, Alexander the Great, and the Romans. By this time, Meroë had become the center of Kushite culture. The temples, the burial pyramids, and other structures at Meroë look Egyptian in many respects—but not all. Some of the temples are devoted to Egyptian deities like Isis, but others pay tribute to local gods. The writing found at Meroë hasn't yet been fully deciphered, but the characters are the letters of an alphabet, not the picture-based hieroglyphics of Egypt. Some people speculate that the writing resembles Greek

From the end of the Egyptian empire to about A.D. 350, when Meroë was conquered by the Ethiopian kingdom of Aksum, life in Kush reflected Sudan's position as a cultural crossroads. The region between the Atbara and Blue Nile rivers—known as the Island of Meroë—was, in those years, a fertile grassland with substantial woodlands and iron ore. The Meroites forged tools and weapons of iron and even carried them east to the Red Sea in hopes of selling them to seaborne traders.

Traveling poets, traders, and soldiers from farther downstream on the Nile introduced Roman culture. But the difficulty of traveling past the northernmost cataract in the Nile prevented Rome from conquering Nubia.

to southern Sudan for slaves. Slavery had existed in Africa, Asia, and Europe for thousands of years, so these slave traders—not all of whom were Arabs or even Muslims—were not doing anything new. But Islam forbids enslavement of Muslims, so Muslim slavers traveled farther afield to find non-Muslim peoples.

Slavers had avoided exploring southern Sudan for four reasons. The cataracts of the Nile hampered navigation. The dry, inhospitable countryside made travel treacherous. Islamic leaders had long focused on the north, which was well known because of earlier Roman and Greek exploration. The local peoples put up fierce resistance to invaders.

Major groups of southern Sudan began moving into their present-day territories in the sixteenth and seventeenth centuries. The Dinka and Nuer might have spread from original homelands in far southwestern Sudan. Other peoples, like the Azande, may have come from somewhere in the Congo River Valley. The Shilluk probably originated in the El Gezira region, just south of where the Blue Nile joins the White Nile, and then moved south and west.

THE OTTOMAN INVASION

The demand for slaves was part of the motivation for a military campaign that would for the first time bring much of Sudan under one government. Since 1250 Egypt had been under the control of the Mamluks, Muslim soldiers of various Central Asian backgrounds. Egypt's rulers had brought Mamluks to Egypt as slaves and had given them spe-

Slavery had existed in Africa, Asia, and Europe for thousands of years, so these slave traders—not all of whom were Arabs or even Muslims—were not doing anything new.

cial military training. The Mamluks eventually took over the government themselves. These Muslims ruled over an Egyptian population that had become partly Arabized.

In 1517 another Central Asian people, the Ottoman Turks, took over Egypt and made it part of their huge

Ottoman Empire. At first the Ottoman rulers let the Mamluks continue to administer Egypt. By the early 1800s, however, Muhammad Ali had become the Ottoman governor of Egypt. Powerful and ruthless, Muhammad Ali purged the Mamluks from their posts, killed as many as he could, and began to expand his influence.

Besides seizing Islam's holy places on the Arabian Peninsula, he decided to send his armies up the Nile to conquer the scattered sultanates and kingdoms of Sudan. He put his son, Ismail, at the head of his forces, which soon took over Nubia and the Funj Sultanate. Ismail was killed soon after the start of this campaign, but the battle continued under other commanders until the Ottoman forces had control of Kordofan.

Ottoman forces also occupied some territory south of the Sudd, mostly the areas near the Nile. In north central

Under the Turkiya, slave raiders captured many Sudanese and took them to encampments, such as this one in Kordofan province, before selling them into bondage.

Independent Picture Service

Muhammad Ahmad ibn al-Sayyid abd Allah claimed to be the Mahdi in 1881. In Arabic, Mahdi means "Islam's awaited guide."

Sudan, the Ottomans set up a fort at the confluence of the two Niles in 1825. In 1826 they named this newly founded settlement Khartoum and made it the capital of Ottoman-ruled Sudan.

The Ottoman troops took what riches they could find. They also enslaved people. The Ottomans valued slaves as signs of success and status, and even administrators in relatively low positions had slaves. The Ottomans taxed the Sudanese people they conquered, and payment of these taxes was often made in slaves. Many male slaves ended up in Muhammad Ali's army, which for a time consisted almost entirely of black African slaves.

The Ottoman regime known as the Turkiya—made up of Turko-Egyptian forces—began in about 1820 and lasted approximately 60 years. The Turkiya imposed its rule southward from the cataracts of the Nile to the hills of Uganda and south-westward to the rim of the Congo River Valley—an area nearly corresponding to the boundaries of modern Sudan. The Turks extended postal service and even telegraph lines to towns like El Obeid, located outside the Nile Valley. They also established military posts at strategic locations as far south as Gondokoro (near modern Juba) and hired non-Muslim Europeans as administrators.

But the Turkiya proved to be weak beyond the most secure lines of supply. Turkish commanders at isolated outposts were at the mercy of local warlords and slavers, who tolerated the Turkiya only as long as it kept open the trade routes for slaves or ivory. In less-isolated areas, the Turks enjoyed cooperation from some of the local ethnic and religious groups, including Islamic brotherhoods such as the Khatmiya.

While Turkish troops were governing Sudan, the British had become more involved in Egypt. In 1875 they had taken control of the Suez Canal, which provided a link between the Mediterranean Sea, the Red Sea, and Britain's Indian empire. The canal cut the distance

Tariqas

Prior to independence, competition for political influence was intense. Tariqas—organizations of Muslims who follow the direction of a particular teacher and are united by their faith and family connections—were among the major vehicles of campaigning. The political parties that emerged at this time typically had a base in or an alliance with at least one tariqa. The major players included the Mahdiya tariqa (of the al-Mahdi family), the Mirghaniya tariqa (of the al-Mirghani family), the Islamic Movement for Liberation (a fundamentalist religious group associated with Egypt's Muslim Brotherhood), and the Ashigga Party (led by Ismail al-Azhari). The Mirghaniya and the Mahdiya had been rivals ever since the early days of the Mahdi's jihad, and the division between these two groups widened into an immense political canyon.

between Britain and India by 6,000 miles.

THE MAHDI

The number of Sudanese who disliked the Turkiya exceeded the number who cooperated with it. The Muslims of northern and central Sudan disliked that these Muslim invaders behaved in un-Islamic ways.

Many Muslims were offended that the Turks employed non-Muslim Europeans as administrators. In 1874 the British soldier Charles Gordon, became one such administrator. Gordon served the Turkiya as a governor in the far south of Sudan, in a province known as Equatoria. In this post, he clashed with the powerful slave trader Zubeir Pasha, who had long served as a government unto himself in the area. Because Gordon prevailed against Zubeir, he became famous in Britain as the man who ended slavery in Sudan. (It is more accurate to say that Gordon limited slavery in Sudan.)

The end of the Turkiya came swiftly, with the rise of a man who claimed to be Islam's long-awaited Mahdi. Islamic tradition held that God would eventually send someone, the Mahdi, to conduct a holy war against evildoers and to bring all who survived to the true way of Islam. In 1881 a Sudanese holy man, Muhammad Ahmad ibn al-Sayyid abd Allah, announced that he was the Mahdi. His followers called themselves the Ansar (helpers), but they have been more commonly known to the outside world as Mahdists.

Based near the east central town of Kosti, the Mahdi soon expanded his influence and became an important charismatic leader. Muslims throughout Sudan, eager to conduct a jihad or holy war against the Turkiya, came to fight on the side of the Mahdi. The Mahdi's forces eventually captured most of north central and west central Sudan. Government troops and administrators who remained had no lines of supply or escape and confined themselves to the few spots left under their control. As the government's soldiers fought back, they hoped a stronger force would come on the scene. The only serious attempt came from Britain.

THE BRITISH TAKE OVER

The British did not consider Egypt part of their empire at

this time, but in every practical sense they had taken over the country by the early 1880s. The Ottoman rulers who officially governed the country had run up huge debts. The British feared that the regime had become too weak and unstable to manage and protect the Suez Canal, a lifeline of British commerce. In 1882 British ships bombarded Alexandria at the mouth of the Nile, and then 20,000 British soldiers landed near the canal. The Ottoman ruler became a mere figurehead, and in the name of Egypt the British devised a plan for dealing with the Mahdi in Sudan. They sent Gordon's military troops to accomplish the task.

When Gordon arrived in Khartoum in February 1884, he raised hopes that the city might repel the Mahdists. In January 1885, however, the Mahdi's followers overran the capital and killed Gordon. British reinforcements arrived too late to prevent a defeat that became legendary—more for its hopelessness than for any great heroism. Gordon's demise drew the attention of the British public, which severely criticized the government in London for not rescuing Khartoum.

Even though the Mahdi

Stock Montage

died soon after his troops captured the capital, the movement held together under Abdullah al-Taishi, who is usually called the Khalifa (meaning "successor"). While the power of the Mahdists was greatest in the north and central areas, they ruled some parts of the south as well. They never actually controlled strong traditional kingdoms like the Fur Sultanate or the Shilluk kingdom. Even where the Mahdists were the uncontested government, their reign was brief and never peaceful.

EUROPEAN RULE

In the late nineteenth century, European countries scrambled for land in Africa. The British, who controlled

The death of General Charles Gordon, depicted under attack in this painting, hit the British hard. They collected money and later opened Khartoum's Gordon College in his honor.

Facing page: *Muhammad Ali recruited black slaves to serve in his army.*

Egypt and held Kenya and Uganda, seemed the most likely European nation to take Sudan. But other powers also had designs on the region. France, in particular, planned to link its holdings in French West Africa to the White Nile by establishing a foothold at a town called Fashoda. This upstream position, from which they could threaten the supply of Nile water to Egypt, would give them great leverage over the British, France's traditional rival.

CHAPTER 2 *The Conflict's Roots*

Under the leadership of General Herbert Horatio Kitchener (later Lord Kitchener), British and Egyptian troops had to fight the Mahdists to subdue Sudan. Besides having far larger armies readily available, the Mahdists were familiar with the territory and knew how to survive in its harshest parts.

But their ambitious holy war had spread the Mahdist troops too thin. The British and Egyptians also had the latest military hardware. The Mahdists suffered defeat after defeat and by 1898, after losing Omdurman, could hold out no longer. Their forces dispersed. Members of the Mahdi's family and other close supporters kept their devotion for him alive in the form of a family-based association that continued to

Archive Photos

After defeating the Mahdists at Omdurman in 1898, Herbert Horatio Kitchener (above) *became the first governor-general of Sudan.*

Independent Picture Service

Left: *British soldiers guard the slain bodies of Mahdist leaders Khalifa Abdullahi and Ahmad Fadil.*

Under the Condominium, the British connected Sudan's northern cities with railroad tracks and telegraph lines. Such developments didn't extend into southern regions, however.

Courtesy of Maryknoll Missioners

be called the Ansar. After the decisive battle of Omdurman, Kitchener went by river steamer to Fashoda, where he encountered the French. Bloodshed was avoided, and the French were eventually compelled to withdraw.

In 1899 the British and Egyptians set up a system of joint control over Sudan. The regime was called the Anglo-Egyptian **Condominium,** which in this context means "joint domain." In practical terms, however, the British really ruled Sudan. British administrators made the decisions, and British officers commanded the troops. Egyptians held low-level administrative posts and made up much of the armed forces.

British influence was strongest in the capital and in other places where there were roads and an administrative **infrastructure.** By building railroads—first to Khartoum, then to Suakin on the Red Sea, and, lastly westward to Kosti and El Obeid— the British slowly brought some previously remote regions of the north within easier reach for commercial and military purposes. In 1906 they opened a new Red Sea port called Port Sudan. The British also installed water-management facilities such as dams and irrigation systems and established vast cotton plantations in the El Gezira to

A generation of African Christian leaders, trained by British missionaries, passed Christianity on to southern Sudanese.

supply British textile mills. Beyond the areas with such infrastructure, Anglo-Egyptian rule probably made little difference. Sudan was still a vast region of isolated villages and oases, where people had little contact with or knowledge of changes within the Khartoum-based government.

MISSIONARIES ARRIVE
In the post-Mahdiya period, however, the south came into greater contact with a particular kind of outsider—the Christian missionary. Catholic missionaries had been operating along the southern reaches of the Nile for about 50 years. Many missionaries were non-British Europeans, like the Slovene Ignaz Knoblecher and the Italian Daniele Comboni. Missionaries led tough lives. Some died from disease or were killed by their former converts, by local religious authorities, or by slave-trading warlords. And they didn't have much luck converting many of the Sudanese to Christianity.

The missionaries set up and operated limited social services in the south, including medical clinics and schools. The education that southerners received in mission schools differed from what was being taught in schools in the north. Missionaries taught classes in English, while northern teachers used Arabic. This presented problems when Sudanese who had been educated in the south wanted to go on to secondary school or college. Because the missionaries only taught through the primary grades, southerners had to pursue further education at English-speaking institutions in present-day Kenya, Uganda, and Tanzania.

The mission effort also posed management problems for the British. To satisfy the various organizations wanting permission to work in southern Sudan, the British authorities finally divided the southern third of the country into spheres of influence among the American Presbyterians, the Roman Catholics, and the Anglicans.

ADMINISTRATIVE CHALLENGES
The British faced two different sets of administrative challenges in Sudan—one in the south and another in the

Missionaries led tough lives. Some died from disease or were killed by their former converts, by local religious authorities, or by slave-trading warlords.

News from the Front

In the summer of 1898, a young Winston Churchill—whose family was well connected in British politics and society—was determined to go to Sudan to participate in the British campaign to overthrow the Mahdist government. Churchill was a second lieutenant in the British army and a reporter for the *Morning Post*.

As rumors began to circulate about the upcoming siege of Sudan, Churchill grew anxious to write about the war and tried to get an assignment. Churchill eventually was posted to the 21st Lancers as a supernumerary—meaning he was an "extra" member of the campaign.

Three weeks following his assignment, Lieutenant Churchill reported to his camp along the Nile. On September 1, 1898, he led a troop of 25 lancers in their first charge at the Battle of Omdurman. Although casualties were high, the British quickly defeated the Mahdist army. In his book, *River War,* Churchill describes the Dervish (Mahdist) surrender. "As soon as it was apparent that the surrender of individuals was accepted, the Dervishes began to come in and lay down their arms—at first by twos and threes, then by dozens, and finally by scores." Remarkably, three days after the first battle charge, Churchill and the 21st Lancers, whose unit had lost about 20 out of 100 men, were on their way home to Britain.

north. In some respects, the southern challenge was more difficult. The south didn't have a central group of leaders to approach or a large army to confront. Instead the British had to deal with many ethnic groups, each resentful of outside rule and interference. Missionaries of different faiths contributed to the chaos. Some missionaries worked with both the British and the southern Sudanese, but because these clerics often came from other European countries, they, too, had their own agendas. Those who didn't agree with British policy may have tried to turn southern-

ers against the government.

As problematic as the situation in the south was, the British saw it as a local military matter to be solved by military means rather than as a deep-rooted threat to the entire regime. In the north, the problems were potentially more threatening. The British were forced to grapple with how to balance Egypt's aspirations in the Condominum, how to deal with rival tariqas and Muslim associations, and how to handle rising **nationalism.**

The British and their Egyptian junior partners ruled Sudan by enlisting the aid of powerful local fac-

tions. For example, the Mahdists, who shared with the British a distrust of Egypt, eventually became supporters of the British. Keeping such allies in the fold required great tact and a lot of attention. As in many of their other colonies, the British hoped to build up a Sudanese civil service so that many local people would have a stake in maintaining the status quo.

Under British rule, the number of educated Sudanese increased (mostly in the Khartoum area). A tradition of education was already strong among the leading Muslim families of Sudan, some of whom sent their sons to Al-Azhar University in Cairo, the Egyptian capital. The aim of this education was religious scholarship.

The British, however, wanted to train students in the more secular skills of civil service and administration. So they established a college in memory of Charles Gordon, and in 1902 Gordon Memorial College (later the University of Khartoum) opened. Contrary to British intentions, the Sudanese men who were the first graduates of Gordon College eventually formed the core of Sudanese nationalists and opposed non-Sudanese rule. Organized into secret societies such as the White Flag League, these young men talked of ousting the British and plotted with Egyptian nationalists.

Their hopes were not met in 1922, when Britain abandoned its protectorate over Egypt and approved the country's independence. Sudan remained under British control. The new British-approved Egyptian constitution failed to claim northern Sudan for Egypt, as many Egyptians and Sudanese would have liked. In 1923—when negotiations between the British and the Egyptians over the fate of northern Sudan failed—nationalist groups in Egypt and northern Sudan rioted. They

> Contrary to British intentions, the Sudanese men who were the first graduates of Gordon College eventually formed the core of Sudanese nationalists and opposed non-Sudanese rule.

staged demonstrations in Khartoum and, in November 1924, the governor-general of Sudan, Sir Lee Stack, was assassinated in Cairo.

Although the British didn't really believe the new Egyptian government had had a part in Stack's death, they wanted to show all nationalist forces in the region who was in charge. They responded by kicking all Egyptian soldiers out of Sudan and by forming the Sudan Defense Force (SDF). It replaced the Egyptian military units that had been stationed in Sudan.

Meanwhile, to further bring things under control, the government closed off the three southern provinces from the north and from the rest of the world. In 1924 a new law called the Closed Districts Ordinance declared southern Sudan off-limits to outsiders. The law also banned the teaching of Arabic and promoted English as the primary language of the south. The division in Sudan between equatorial south and Islamic north had always existed, but this was the first time the government had made it official policy.

ROAD TO INDEPENDENCE

While Britain tightened its control of the region, pro-independence groups continued to work toward their goal. Over time the British agreed on a gradual move toward independence for Sudan. During the Second World War (1939–1945), the British set up the Advisory Council for Northern Sudan and in 1948 established a legislative assembly. The assembly, however, had very little power—the most it could do was advise the British governor.

Pro-independence groups dominated the legislative elections, especially after the pro-Egyptian National Unionist Party (NUP) staged a boycott. Some southerners were elected to the assembly and were able to gain some experience of British-style parliamentary democracy. Elections in 1953 produced a parliament that began operating in 1954. The NUP—the party associated with the Mirghaniya tariqa—won a solid majority and began preparing to take over full governing authority from the British.

Like the 1948 legislative assembly, the 1954 parliament included representatives from the south. The largest southern party was the Southern Liberal Party, composed mostly of educated southerners, many of whom had been civil servants. These southerners had

no interest in the political intrigues among Muslim factions, but the issue of whether Sudan would unite with Egypt meant something to them. They didn't support this move.

The southerners, who numbered only 22 out of the more than 300 delegates to parliament, also quickly saw that even without a Sudan-Egypt union the non-Muslim peoples of Sudan would have only a small voice in post-British Sudan. When Muslim enthusiasm for Islamic education or sharia came up, the non-Muslim legislators realized the immensity of the support for these causes.

At the same time, the Khartoum government had already been dealing with another revolt in the south. Southern soldiers of a Juba-

The newly elected Sudan Parliament met in Khartoum for the first time on January 1, 1954. The British governor-general (seated, front and center) presided over the meeting.

based army unit mutinied on August 18, 1955, to protest what they saw as unfair domination by the north. When the riot was over, 300 northern officials and civilians had been killed. The government suppressed the revolt and executed 70 southerners for challenging government authority. But many rebels took their guns and escaped into the bush, where they organized to fight a civil war.

INDEPENDENCE

The Sudanese parliament declared Sudan's independence on December 19, 1955. On January 1, 1956, Ismail al-Azhari of the NUP, the prime minister, presided over independence day celebrations. His government did not push for union with Egypt, and the issue eventually lost support.

On New Year's Day in 1956, Prime Minister Ismail al-Azhari and opposition leader Muhammed Ahmad Mahjub looked on as the flag of independent Sudan was hoisted for the first time.

Independent Picture Service

General Ibrahim Abboud, commander of the Sudanese army and leader of the 1958 coup, shook hands with his new staff members after the military takeover.

Parliamentary rule, which was distinguished more by factional bickering and bribery than by national development, didn't last long. Soon antigovernment demonstrators protested the government's inability to take action to solve Sudan's social, economic, and political problems. Egypt even suggested that it might support a coup (swift overthrow) against the Sudanese government.

In November 1958, a general named Ibrahim Abboud staged the first of Sudan's military coups in conjunction with Umma Party (UP) members and two other army generals. Abboud was against political parties because he claimed that they only served personal ambitions. He dismissed the parliament and ruled by decree through a council of 12 military officers. Abboud's strong-arm rule improved the economy somewhat. He managed to settle water disputes with Egypt. His policies benefited from a successful cotton crop during his first year in office.

But Abboud's policies also brought southern discontent to the boiling point. Beginning in 1962, the government outlawed expressions of religious and cultural differences in the south and pushed to Arabize the entire country. The Muslim-dominated government began kicking out the Christian missionaries, replacing mission schools with Islamic schools. Teachers at Islamic schools taught in Arabic, which most southerners could not speak.

With these moves, the Abboud regime put more pressure on the south to conform to Islamic standards. The government enforced the new rules by beefing up its military presence in the south. With soldiers patrolling their villages and observing their daily business, southerners felt as if they were living in occupied territory. Many disaffected southerners left the country to establish opposition groups, such as the Sudan African National Union (SANU). Other **dissidents** stayed in Sudan and set up military resistance organizations in anticipation of civil war. Anya Nya, the most prominent group, was founded in 1963.

The government continued to commit more military resources to the south and to accuse missionaries of dividing the region. The Abboud regime finally expelled all missionaries and closed all missionary schools. But its troubles were not limited to the south. In October 1964, groups of students in the north led a general uprising to protest the government's lack of action on economic and educational reform. The northern opposition eventually forced Abboud to resign. Sirr al Khatim al Khalifa, a nonpolitical senior civil servant, became prime minister in the transitional government.

There was some hope after this October Revolution that the civil war could be

AP/Wide World Photos

resolved. Some southern leaders helped govern the country until a new legislature could be elected. The southern resistance settled down somewhat, and new legislative elections were held in 1965. The Umma Party, which had long been associated with the Mahdists, won 75 out of 158 parliamentary seats. It led a coalition (combination of parties) in this legislature. The UP and coalition leader Muhammed Ahmad Mahjub had two goals—to solve the southern problem and to remove **Communists** from positions of power. Shortly after taking power, Mahjub's government sent troops to southern Sudan. Southerners reported that the Sudanese army set fire to churches and homes, closed schools, and destroyed crops and cattle. Thousands of

Facing page: Along with several non-African nations, many neighboring countries, such as Ethiopia and Eritrea, disliked Sudan's Islamic regime. They supplied southern rebels with guns and ammunition. In 1967 this group of Anya Nya officers posed with captured Chinese weapons.

southerners fled. By the late 1960s, about 500,000 Sudanese had died. Hundreds of thousands of others had flooded refugee camps in neighboring countries. In 1966 the UP split. Mahjub's faction opposed the party majority, which was under the leadership of Sadiq al-Mahdi, the great-grandson of the Mahdi and one of the party's rising political stars. He served temporarily as Sudan's prime minister. As Sudanese leadership crumbled, efforts to solve the country's basic problems of food, water, and ongoing conflict became secondary.

NIMEIRI TAKES OVER

Long-term change came to Sudan in May 1969 when a group of junior officers, among them Colonel Jaafar Mohammed Nimeiri, staged yet another military coup. At first there was little resentment in Sudan at the loss of representative democracy and the return of military dictatorship. After the do-little government of the 1965–1969 parliament, the Sudanese seemed eager for stronger leadership. Nimeiri became president of Sudan in 1971, by which time his

regime had survived an attempted overthrow by members of the Sudanese Communist Party and had suppressed the Mahdists.

By 1972 it had become easier for the government and the southern rebels to negotiate. In the past, there had been so many southern rebel groups that the Sudanese government had had trouble gathering them together to talk about peace. But as power in the north fell into Nimeiri's hands, a general named Joseph Lagu united several southern groups under one umbrella organization—the Southern Sudan Liberation Movement (SSLM). Most important, the SSLM encompassed Anya Nya, the strongest of the many rebel militias in the south.

The SSLM and the Nimeiri government signed a historic peace deal in February 1972 called the Addis Ababa Agreement, after the Ethiopian capital city where the two groups met. Among other things, the government and the SSLM agreed that the south could function as one unit instead of as three separate provinces (Bahr al-Ghazal, Upper Nile, and Equatoria). The terms also

Coup d'etat

In the photo above, President Nimeiri personally questions Lieutenant Colonel Babakr Al Nour *(far right, standing)* about his involvement in the 1971 coup attempt.

Another person accused of involvement in the 1971 coup attempt was a Dinka named Joseph Garang, a southerner who belonged to the Sudanese Communist Party and who in 1969 had been appointed Minister for Southern Affairs in Nimeiri's government. Garang had come up with a plan for regional autonomy—self-rule, but not complete independence for the south. His plan outlived him. Garang was executed in prison in 1971 for his alleged part in the coup, but his regional autonomy proposal formed the basis for a landmark agreement between the Khartoum government and the southern rebels.

forces would gradually merge with the Sudanese army.

Although not a perfect agreement, the Addis Ababa accord did calm most of the fighting for a while. For the next nine years, as the government enacted many of the agreement's proposals, Sudan experienced its first period of relative peace since independence. In 1974 residents of the south elected a regional assembly that began exercising authority over a newly unified south.

Nimeiri took advantage of the respite to push ahead with some development projects and to seek international grants for them. The International Monetary Fund (IMF) paid for some of the projects, and the newly rich oil regimes of the Arabian Peninsula picked up the tab for others. But many of the projects seemed to benefit only the north. For example, the Jonglei Canal project which would allow water of the White Nile to bypass the swamps of the Sudd—appeared to be a positive step for the southern economy. But environmentalists claimed that the damage caused by the project to the south's ecology would out-

said the south could help police itself, could have its own regional government to handle local affairs, and would get government money to support its **autonomous** institutions. The government also agreed to help bring back

the hundreds of thousands (perhaps as many as a million) of southern Sudanese who had fled the fighting between the army and the rebels. The rebels agreed that Sudan should remain united and that the rebel

weigh any economic benefits. In fact, the project seemed best for northerners, who would enjoy increased water flows on the Nile.

Southerners were also upset that the government never bothered to consult them about the canal. When the U.S.-based company Chevron began pumping oil from the Bentiu region in southern Sudan in the early 1970s, the government again planned to channel the rich resource north. Instead of opening an oil refinery in Bentiu, the central government decided to pipe the oil to a facility in the northern town of Kosti, depriving the south of employment opportunities and profits.

It seemed that Nimeiri's ideas were better than his management skills. Many of the projects limped along under lax ministries more interested in attracting money than in completing projects. With big projects producing little return and with the need to begin paying back the lenders who had made the projects possible, Sudan sank deeper into debt. To raise more cash, the government increased the official prices of some basic goods, prompting riots by students and by outraged consumers.

NIMEIRI'S ISLAMIZATION PLAN

As Nimeiri saw his northern support waver, he enacted new legislation attractive to Islamic groups. But his new alliances didn't win Nimeiri friends elsewhere. In 1973 and 1974, several groups tried to overthrow the government. Nimeiri responded to the unrest by jailing numerous dissidents and by declaring a state of emergency.

As Nimeiri's popularity fell during the late 1970s, Islamic fundamentalism in Sudan and in other Muslim countries was on the rise. A Sudanese lawyer named Hassan al-Turabi headed the movement. Turabi had spent much of the 1950s and early 1960s outside Sudan. He had attended schools in London and Paris and had strong ties to the Muslim Brotherhood, an Islamic activist movement based in Egypt. When he returned to Sudan in 1965, Turabi began uniting the Muslim Brotherhood with the country's other like-minded groups. Eventually, the enlarged organization led by Turabi became known as the National Islamic Front (NIF).

Although religious conservatives had opposed Nimeiri in earlier days, he chose to support the Islamist position that government and society should be organized according to Islamic principles. In 1977 Nimeiri gave Turabi the important government post of attorney general. Members of the NIF and the Muslim Brotherhood gained power within the civil service and in socially important fields like education.

Meanwhile, political movements in the south appeared to be gaining supporters. When several southern military units mutinied in May 1983, the government took action. Despite southern protests, Nimeiri attempted to thwart southern gains by once again dividing the region into three provinces. This action clearly violated the Addis Ababa Agreement. A few months later the government initiated plans to ban alcohol in Sudan and gradually to promote an entirely Islamic society. The Addis Ababa Agreement was falling apart, and, in September 1983, Nimeiri dealt a death blow to the accord by deciding to reform Sudanese law immediately according to sharia. ⊕

CHAPTER

3

THE PRESENT CONFLICT

When the government imposed nationwide sharia, called the September Laws, full-scale civil war broke out in the south. John Garang, the commander of one of the military units that had mutinied in May, formed the Sudanese People's Liberation Army (SPLA) and its allied political wing, the Sudanese People's Liberation Movement (SPLM). The SPLA was a predominantly Dinka force, but it attracted other disaffected southerners as well. Many of its members were former soldiers who had taken their weapons and ammunition with them when they had turned against the government.

The rebels seemed to be well supplied with guns and ammunition. They not only managed huge military operations that threatened to capture even the southern capital of Juba, but they also set up a radio station that broadcast in Arabic and English. The Sudanese government accused Libya and Ethiopia, both of which had very poor relations with the Nimeiri regime, of supporting the rebels. When jets bombed Omdurman in 1984, the government blamed Libya.

Meanwhile, Nimeiri's troubles at home only got worse. During 1984 and 1985, the southern conflict escalated. Physicians and university professors went on strike. Every school in Khartoum closed for more than a month because of urban unrest when demonstrators protested the rising costs of food, gas, and transportation. The general strikes shut down the country while Nimeiri was on a visit to the United States.

Nimeiri had tried to stem political opposition by im-prisoning or sometimes even executing potential rivals. He arrested Sadiq al-Mahdi, the ex-UP prime minister, for opposing Islamization after the September Laws were declared. Nimeiri ordered the execution of Mahmoud Mohamad Taha, a prominent Islamic scholar. Al-Turabi didn't wait for Nimeiri to initiate a rift. He distanced himself from the faltering president by resigning from the government in early 1985.

Facing page: *The most recent bouts of violence have exploded in eastern Sudan along the Eritrean and Ethiopian borders. In the past, both countries have supported the rebel troops.*

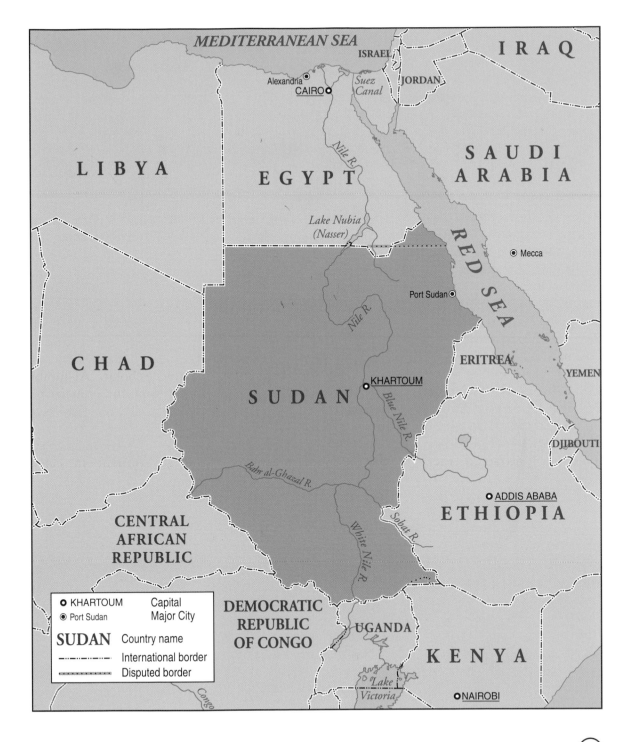

When Nimeiri realized that southern opposition groups would not live peacefully under sharia, he tried to repeal the September Laws, saying that sharia would not be applied in the south. But it was too late. Southern militias were already advancing quickly, seizing vast tracts of southern territory from the government. By then the SPLA was in control of two of the country's three southern provinces.

ANOTHER PARLIAMENT

Later that year while Nimeiri was out of the country in 1985, Sudanese labor unions brought the economy to a halt over inflated grain prices. The army under General Abdul Rahman Suar el-Dahab was forced to overthrow Nimeiri and take control of Sudan. (Nimeiri later went into exile in Egypt.) Suar el-Dahab scheduled parliamentary elections for 1986. He and the Transitional Military Council (TMC), advisers that included some southerners, ruled for about a year in the interim.

For a while, there seemed to be some hope that tensions would be eased. The SPLA announced a short truce, and Anya Nya II, an-

Reuters/ Corbis-Bettmann

other southern militia, agreed to talk to the government about ending the war. The TMC promised not to apply sharia harshly.

The elections in April 1986 gave the UP enough votes to form the next government, so Sadiq al Mahdi again became prime minister. Aware of the damage done by Nimeiri's attempts to impose sharia, al-Mahdi pledged not to apply it, a pledge that cost him the support of the NIF.

Al-Mahdi's government was a practical, down-to-business operation, without the doctrinal agenda that had characterized Nimeiri's regime. But the administration had its hands full trying to deal with the impact of the civil war, in which the SPLA was making significant progress.

Facing page: *On April 11, 1985, young Sudanese filled the streets of Khartoum to celebrate the ousting of Colonel Jaafar al-Nimeiri.*

© Caroline Penn/ Panos Pictures

Women living in Khartoum's Al Sahafa neighborhood, an area known for its strong support of Hassan al-Turabi, stood in line to cast their votes in the April 1986 elections.

In addition, a severe drought that threatened the lives of more than two million Sudanese posed another problem. The government was funneling any money it had into fighting the southern rebellion. As a result, international aid became a matter of life or death for many Sudanese. Yet supplying food to the inhabitants of a war zone was not easy. The Khartoum government sometimes charged aid workers with aiding the rebels and banned Red Cross flights to the southern part of Sudan. Meanwhile, rebel forces threatened aid workers and hoarded food for themselves.

In the late 1980s, the government accused the NIF of stirring up occasional anti-government riots—even though some of these protests were probably spontaneous explosions of anger over Sudan's chronic shortages of affordable food. Famine conditions intensified in 1988, when floods destroyed Sudanese crops. As devastating as they were, the floods had one redeeming factor—they finally drew the attention of the international media, which had been

Left: *A Sudanese police officer drives back a hungry crowd as they attempt to reach the relief grain donated by Save the Children.* Below: *Operation Lifeline trucks deliver much-needed relief food.*

ignoring conditions in Sudan to focus on famines in nearby Ethiopia and Somalia. More and more Sudanese were starving, and the government seemed unable to do much about it.

In March 1988, a UN emergency plan called Operation Lifeline was formulated. The plan was to deliver more than 100,000 tons of food and supplies to two million starving people in central and southern Sudan. But most of the shipment remained in railway cars, where it rotted after the government banned traffic to the south. When the UN at-tempted to deliver grain in trucks from Kenya, bandits—suspected of being SPLA operatives—attacked and killed the drivers.

Seven months later, one of the worst of Khartoum's riots highlighted the deepening rift between NIF fundamentalists and the less-radical parties running Sudan. Prime Minis-ter al-Mahdi had declared his support for a plan, put forward by his NUP rival Mohammed Osman el-Mirghani, to quell southern unrest. The plan involved lifting the application of sharia in southern Sudan. The NIF—which opposed any concessions to the south-erners and believed that aid

aid agencies and Christian churches were working with southerners—attacked southern opposition group demonstrators in the capital on November 22, 1988. Five British aid workers died in the crossfire. Fed up with NIF outbursts, the government expelled Turabi from all governmental posts in 1989. Once again, he went into opposition.

AL-BASHIR'S COUP

In July 1989, a group of army officers calling themselves the Revolutionary Command Council (RCC) seized power under the leadership of Brigadier General Omar Hassan Ahmad al-Bashir. Sadiq al-Mahdi was arrested within a few days. Over the next few weeks, other members of the traditional ruling elites, including el-Mirghani, also found themselves in prison.

The real power behind al-Bashir and the RCC, however, was Turabi and the NIF. The party purged the civil service and universities of people who disagreed with NIF policies. The NIF also organized militias. Some of them operated as a sort of civilian army called the Popular Defense Force (PDF) that

Hassan al-Turabi

The real power behind Sudan's government is the leader of the National Islamic Front, Hassan al-Turabi. He is highly educated, articulate, and persuasive. He's also firmly committed to making Islam the controlling force in the lives of all Sudanese, whether they are Muslim or not.

Turabi was born in the early 1930s in eastern Sudan. His father was an *ustaz* (religious teacher) who deeply instilled the tenets of Islam into young Hassan. Notably clever and quick-witted, Hassan al-Turabi was sent to Khartoum University to study law in 1951. There, he became interested in the Muslim Brotherhood, a group of young Egyptian and Sudanese Islamists (people who believe that Islamic law should govern society).

After earning his law degree, he went to Europe. He spent several years studying in London and then Paris, where he earned his Ph.D. at the Sorbonne. When he returned to Sudan in 1964, his main goal was to promote the cause of the Muslim Brotherhood, a group Turabi eventually led. Since then, Turabi has been a practicing lawyer, the dean of law at Khartoum University (in the 1970s), Sudan's attorney general (in the 1980s), and speaker of the parliament (in the late 1990s). The government's push toward further Islamization of society has benefited Turabi throughout his career.

Reuters/ Corinne Dufka/ Archive Photos

After a fierce battle with Sudanese government troops near the Ugandan border in February 1995, SPLA soldiers pass the remains of a government soldier. In the early 1990s, government troops launched an offensive to push the SPLA from its southern stronghold.

worked hand in hand with the official army to subdue rebellious southern villages.

Later that year, the new government offered a cease-fire to the rebel troops fighting for the south. Although fighting did drop off for a few months, the southern leaders placed no trust in al-Bashir's government. Garang's branch of the SPLA wanted a unified Sudan under secular rule. Al-Bashir's NIF-inspired government, on the other hand, would settle for nothing less than a strictly Islamic government.

THE SPLA SPLITS

In the early 1990s, the power of the SPLA was diffused when the group split into several factions. The main reason for the split was disagreement over whether the group should fight for a united Sudan under secular leadership or for an independent south.

One of the breakaway leaders was Riek Machar, who became head of the Southern Sudan Defense Force (SSDF), a coalition of anti-Garang rebel groups. These breakaway groups

began working with al-Bashir's government against Garang and his factions, forming an unusual group of "pro-government rebels." Such alliances developed because many in the Khartoum government favored giving Machar's group what it wanted—the south's **secession** from Sudan.

Another event dealt a tremendous blow to the SPLA. In August 1991, the Ethiopian regime that had been supporting the SPLA fell from power. The SPLA scrambled for resources.

Riek Machar, leader of the SSIM and government-appointed head of the SCC

Below: *John Garang, SPLA chair*

Rebels Battle One Another

Competition among rebel groups has sometimes led to actual combat. In August 1997, the government appointed SSIM leader Riek Machar president of a new body called the Southern Coordination Council. It was supposed to manage affairs in the south until a vote on the area's political future could be held in 2001. Expecting that Machar would set up his administration in the town of Juba, John Garang's forces began targeting Juba's northern outskirts, hoping to disrupt connections between Machar and the north.

Internal divisions and the loss of outside support took their toll on the organization. Within two years, the SPLA had lost significant ground in the south. The government regained 90 percent of the land in the south including all major towns.

At the same time, violence against non-Arab and non-Muslim ethnic groups became a serious problem under al-Bashir's regime. Reports began circulating that an armed group of civilians identifying themselves as Arabs had massacred 600 Shilluk people just north of where the Bahr al-Ghazal joins the White Nile. The reports said soldiers of the regular army witnessed the killings but had done nothing to stop them. Other reports documented a 1993 government campaign in which the army and the PDF militias worked together to move Nuba people from their villages and into Islamic re-education camps. The troops killed hundreds of Nuba people who refused to cooperate on the spot.

BAD RELATIONS

Sudan's Islamization policies further isolated the country from the rest of the world. Throughout the 1990s, the United States severely criticized Sudan for its alleged support for terrorism. Rich Arab countries like Saudi Arabia, which had previously assisted Sudan financially, despised Sudan for its support

International Currents

One major complaint by dissidents is that al-Bashir's government has poorly managed the international currents that tug at Sudan. The country's handling of the conflict between Islamic fundamentalism and secular models of government is a case in point. Fundamentalist Islam has drawn al-Bashir into its orbit. Iran sees Sudan as an excellent staging point for its opposition to Egypt's secular government, which Iran dislikes for having made peace with Israel and for not instituting sharia. Sudan also has potential as a military base. Iran has reportedly made arrangements to position naval forces near Port Sudan.

In trying to satisfy its foreign friends, Sudan's government has sheltered people whom some other nations, including the United States, accuse of terrorism. The U.S. government's diplomatic relations with Sudan are decidedly strained. In 1996 the United States moved its embassy out of Sudan to a temporary location in Kenya. Many times the United States has accused Sudan of sponsoring terrorism and has threatened boycotts and aid cutoffs.

In August 1998, for example, a terrorist group with ties to Sudan led by an Islamic fundamentalist named Osama bin Laden claimed responsibility for the bombings of U.S. embassies in Kenya and Tanzania. The bombings killed nearly 300 Kenyans and Tanzanians and 12 Americans. The United States retaliated by firing cruise missiles at a chemical plant in Khartoum, believed to be manufacturing chemical weapons, and at an alleged terrorist training camp in Afghanistan. The Sudanese government maintained its innocence throughout the ordeal, claiming that the chemical plant manufactured medication, not weapons.

Sudanese voters study an election poster for President Omar al-Bashir. The government banned all opposition parties, so al-Bahir faced almost no competition for reelection.

of Iraq during the Gulf War. (In the war, Iraq attacked Saudi territory.) The UN imposed sanctions on Sudan for human-rights violations. Last but not least, international aid donors blacklisted Sudan because the country had a combined debt of more than $15 billion.

Despite this desperate situation, Sudan's warring parties would not make any serious effort to resolve their differences. In 1994 an African organization called the Inter-Governmental Authority on Development (IGAD)—made up of Kenya, Ethiopia, Uganda, Eritrea, Somalia, Sudan, and Djibouti—arranged for the Sudanese government and the southern rebel leaders to meet. Mediators formulated a statement of principles. These included declarations that Sudan should keep religion separate from politics and that it should allow other political parties to grow strong enough to compete with the NIF. Al-Bashir's government rejected the agreement. Both sides stood their ground and would not budge.

The government held elections in 1996 to bring new members to the National Assembly (Sudan's legislature). No international groups monitored the proceedings, so there's no reliable independent assessment of how free and fair the elections were. The NIF won most of the seats, and Turabi became the speaker of the assembly. In the contest for the presidency, Bashir—the only

Neighborhood Disputes

In June 1995, President Hosni Mubarak of Egypt went to Addis Ababa, Ethiopia's capital, for a meeting of the Organization of African Unity. He narrowly escaped with his life when three gunmen opened fire, killing some of his bodyguards. Blame immediately fell on Sudanese agents and the government of President al-Bashir in Khartoum. Egypt charged that Sudan had planned the attempt, had aided the attackers, and was giving them refuge. A UN investigation later supported Egypt's claims and passed a resolution demanding that Sudan send the suspects to Ethiopia for trial. Sudan claimed not to know where the suspects were.

Two years later, at a meeting of Africa's Inter-Governmental Authority on Development (IGAD) in Kenya, Sudan was accused of aiding yet another assassination attempt. This time the charge was made by Isaias Afewerki, the president of Eritrea. Afewerki said that a Sudanese hit man plotting to assassinate him had been discovered a month earlier in Eritrea's capital city of Asmara. Hearing the charges, Sudan's al-Bashir grew incensed, scribbled out a note, and then handed it to Afewerki, who later said that it was "full of insults."

Ugandan army soldiers watch over the Ugandan schoolgirls abducted by the Lord's Resistance Army.

Meanwhile, another neighbor—President Yuweri Museveni of Uganda—had boycotted the IGAD meeting because al-Bashir was there. Museveni was angry because of a dispute involving 112 Sudanese soldiers and 21 Ugandan schoolgirls. The soldiers had been captured a few months earlier on Ugandan territory, supposedly while aiding the Lord's Resistance Army (LRA), a group of Ugandan rebels. The teenage girls were the remnant of a group of 139 kidnapped the previous October from St. Mary's Girls' School in northern Uganda by the LRA. The LRA was holding the girls at a camp in southern Sudan, where they reportedly enjoyed the support of the Sudanese government. Sudan had promised to get the LRA to return the 21 girls if Uganda would return the 112 soldiers. Suddenly, however, al-Bashir claimed not to know where the girls were. Museveni did not believe it and refused to go to any meeting involving al-Bashir.

candidate representing a major political party (the NIF)—won with about three-fourths of the vote. His opponents charged that the result was a sham, characterized by widespread intimidation of voters.

CONTINUED RESISTANCE
Meanwhile, on April 21, 1997, relations between the major players took an unexpected turn when representatives of the NIF and the SSIM signed a peace agreement. The agreement maintained that sharia would remain the source for all legislation. General laws would apply to all states, but states would have the right to pass accompanying laws on specific matters.

The two groups agreed that Sudan should be a democracy in which all citizens have basic freedoms. The agreement established a four-year period of transition to a democratic system. During that time, a 25-member council would coordinate interaction between the southern states. By the end of the four-year period, the southern Sudanese would decide in a public vote whether to secede from the north or to remain part of Sudan. Finally, the agreement pledged to reconstruct, rehabilitate, repatriate, and redevelop the southern areas affected by the war.

Garang's rebel forces rejected the peace agreement because it included a public vote on the south's independence. The SPLA chose to have nothing to do with any discussions on southern secession. Nevertheless, the NIF and SSIM began to implement it. The government announced a new Southern Coordination Council that Machar would lead. The council fully expected SPLA forces to attempt to disrupt its operations.

Meanwhile, the SPLA found new backers. Under the banner of the Cairo-based National Democratic Alliance (NDA), disaffected northerners like DUP leader el-Mirghani joined forces with Garang's faction of the SPLA to end al-Bashir's regime. In the late 1990s, the NDA fighters gained

Reuters/ Jeremiah Kamau/ Archive Photos

SPLA troops defend the town of Mundri against government advances. After four hours of fighting, the town remained under SPLA control.

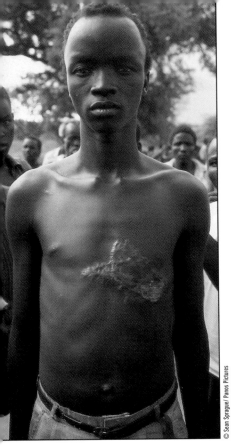

A victim of torture by burning shows his scars. Pushed from his home by the civil war, he lives in a displacement camp.

towns, although Garang's faction of the SPLA captured Rumbek in the west and began to exert pressure on the government's supply lines north of Juba.

The bouts of fighting were punctuated by efforts to achieve peace. At an IGAD meeting in the Kenyan capital of Nairobi in 1997, al-Bashir seemed to agree to the principles set forth at the 1994 IGAD meeting. His sudden agreement surprised many onlookers. Hopes for a breakthrough were dashed, however, when al-Bashir said shortly afterward that he had been misunderstood. He didn't really support these principles, and he meant to say only that they could be a basis for discussion.

In August of the same year, South African president Nelson Mandela stepped in to mediate the Sudanese conflict. Al-Bashir met with Mandela, who had also been in contact with Garang. Rumors began circulating that Mandela might be able to entice Garang to talk with al-Bashir in Kenya. Mandela's efforts fell flat when Garang claimed he could not attend meetings at the scheduled times.

So the civil war continued, and al-Bashir's regime remained in place through 1998. Government forces hold major cities and towns, while southern rebel groups patrol the bush. Neither side seems to be gaining any ground, yet they both refuse to compromise. Although northern moderates, weary of war, have been prepared to negotiate peace even if it means giving up the south, the NIF's commitment to making Sudan a thoroughly Islamic society appears unshaken. The government hopes that the agreement reached with Machar in April 1997 will work out. Garang's group remains just as determined to fight for a united Sudan, free from Islamic rule. ⊕

territory near the Ethiopian and Eritrean borders. This location put them within striking distance of the Blue Nile town of Damazin, the location of a vital hydroelectric plant. But they had yet to attack the dam or any other strategic installation in the east. In the south, the government continued to hold Juba and the other major

Facing page: About two thirds of Sudan is considered the north. The Bahr al-Ghazal and the Sobat River create a rough boundary between the north and the south.

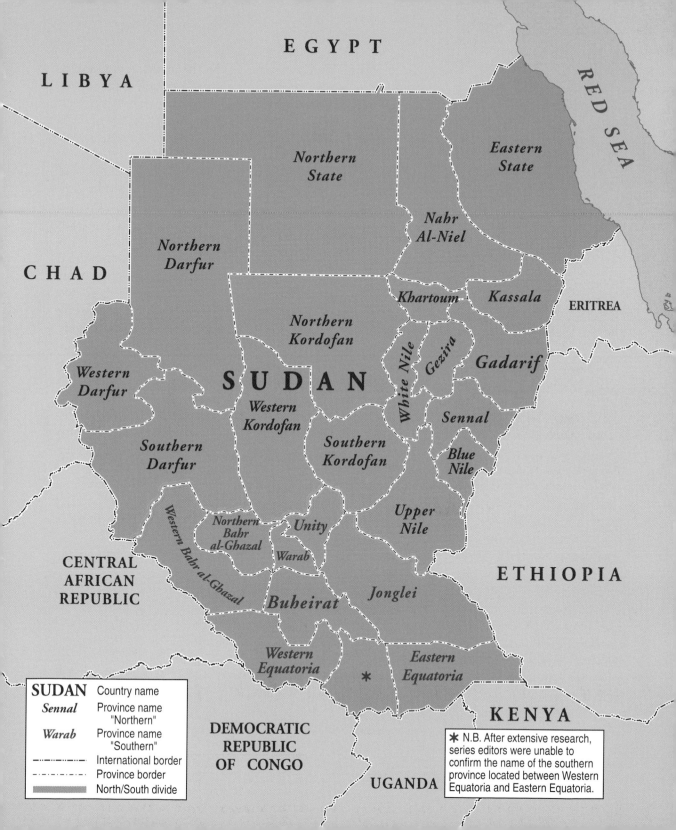

EGYPT

LIBYA

RED SEA

CHAD

Northern
State

Eastern
State

Northern
Darfur

Nahr
Al-Niel

Khartoum

Kassala

ERITREA

Western
Darfur

Northern
Kordofan

SUDAN

White Nile

Gezira

Gadarif

Western
Kordofan

Sennal

Southern
Darfur

Southern
Kordofan

Blue
Nile

Western Bahr al-Ghazal

Northern
Bahr
al-Ghazal

Unity

Upper
Nile

ETHIOPIA

CENTRAL
AFRICAN
REPUBLIC

Warab

Buheirat

Jonglei

Western
Equatoria

*

Eastern
Equatoria

KENYA

DEMOCRATIC
REPUBLIC
OF CONGO

UGANDA

SUDAN	Country name
Sennal	Province name "Northern"
Warab	Province name "Southern"
–·–·–	International border
···········	Province border
▬	North/South divide

✳ N.B. After extensive research,
series editors were unable to
confirm the name of the southern
province located between Western
Equatoria and Eastern Equatoria.

4

WHAT'S BEING DONE TO SOLVE THE PROBLEM

In reality, there are several problems that need to be solved simultaneously for peace to come to Sudan. One of the questions is whether and how Muslims and non-Muslims can live peacefully together. Other pressing issues include alleviating the country's extreme poverty and finding a stable governmental system. The magnitude of these problems is discouraging to many observers. Although no solution has worked yet, efforts continue.

THE STALEMATE

Al-Bashir's government holds fast to the agreement reached with the SSIM in April 1997. This deal would provide for a southern vote on whether to remain a part of Sudan. The present government appears to have little sympathy for the political aspirations of non-Muslims in Sudan. Sharing true power on a national level with southern Christians or followers of local religions would conflict with the NIF's goal of an Islamic social system in Sudan. Like presidents and dictators before him, al-Bashir has proposed autonomy for the south. Recent government efforts have implied a possible secession of the south from Sudan.

But whether Sudan's government would allow a truly independent southern nation is questionable. This new southern state would theoretically be able to control the life-giving waters of the White Nile, as it flows northward through Sudan toward the Mediterranean Sea. Furthermore, the only significant oil reserves yet discovered in Sudan are within territory that would almost certainly secede. Many doubt that Khartoum's insecure, impoverished government would actually cut loose such resources.

Garang and the part of the SPLA still loyal to him would certainly refuse to recognize the independence of the south and would oppose it militarily. These anti-separatist forces have support from the dispos-

With the war at a standstill, neither side expects Sudan's divisions to be erased by military force.

sessed old-line parties and tariqas whose leaders are currently partners in the NDA.

With the war at a standstill, neither side expects Sudan's divisions to be erased by military force. The government of one of Africa's poorest nations cannot afford continuing conflict. Even with the addition of pro-government rebels and even with the quasimilitary PDF, the Sudanese army is stretched very thin. With the new eastern front that the NDA opened up near Ethiopia and Eritrea, the government's military situation has gotten even worse. But the rebels haven't been able to overwhelm the army either. Defections within the SPLA have stalled the rebels's ability to concentrate enough force on vital installations.

A new government seems to be a necessity to any workable solution that keeps Sudan united. Only a regime less committed to Islamization could include the southerners as equals or earn their trust. But that seems unlikely in the near future. As long as Turabi's NIF remains powerful, no president in Sudan could survive long without supporting an Islamic state.

Reuters/ George Mulala/Archive Photos

John Garang

John Garang, leader of the SPLA, has been described as charming, smart, and even funny. Armed with a Ph.D. from Iowa State University, Garang approaches the conflict in Sudan with some definite ideas about how the country should be run. And they don't mesh with the way things stand at present. He regards the southern problem as an ethnic one, but he also believes that Sudan's problems should take a back seat to the necessity of progress. According to Garang, uneven development is the cause of the current tensions. The north needs the resources in the south to sustain any kind of effective economy, and the south requires the north's access to the sea to move its products to markets around the world. The south also lacks the national entity required to govern the region. For these reasons, Garang sees regional autonomy for the south within the nation of Sudan as the only option. He has made it clear through military force that he will accept no other system.

INTERNATIONAL EFFORTS

In early 1989, before al-Bashir took power, the United States offered to bring the warring sides together for peace talks. Former President Jimmy Carter, acting as a private citizen, went to Sudan later that year to attempt a settlement. He got nowhere. The government's insistence on enforcing sharia stood in the way. Carter had better luck on another mission in 1995, when he managed to negotiate a two-month cease-fire but nothing more.

The UN, for which Sudan's hungry people and displaced refugees are a major expense, has also tried its hand at brokering a peace. For example, in 1995 the UN Educational, Scientific, and Cultural Organization (UNESCO) launched a program called Culture of Peace to lessen tensions in Sudan. Other than a few informal meetings between leaders of Sudanese factions, nothing much came of the effort.

UN peacemaking has had little effect because Sudan has bad relations even with the United Nations. There is ill will regarding Sudan's human-rights record. For example, a 1994 report by a special UN investigator, Gaspar Biro, criticized not only the government but all sides involved in Sudan's conflict for ruthlessly exposing civilians to harm and for exploiting them in pursuit of battle gains. The Sudanese government took special offense when this report led the UN General Assembly to formally censure Sudan. Later reports were no more complimentary. They publicly accused Sudan's government forces of rape, kidnapping, and slavery.

HELP FROM THE NEIGHBORS

Some of Sudan's neighbors, including a few of those with whom Sudan has terrible relations, have made the most progress on solving Sudan's problems. With forces right on Sudan's borders, the most hostile neighbors can attract the country's attention in ways that more distant powers never could. IGAD arranged several negotiating sessions between the rebels and the Khartoum government, many of which had to be called off when one party or another refused to attend.

Given the cross-border raiding and ill will between Sudan and some of its neighbors, a violent end to the problem is a possibility.

AIDING THE HUNGRY AND THE HOMELESS

As the conflict rages on, hunger and homelessness afflict increasing numbers of Sudanese. Many groups have attempted to stem these problems, while other groups have worked toward a peaceful resolution to the conflict. The Sudanese government, in dire financial straits and having angered nearly every large potential donor, can do little to help its own citizens. The government does operate a Relief and Development Agency that is supposed to deal with problems of poverty and substandard living conditions. But this organization is most active among the Muslim populations in government-controlled regions of Sudan. It has had little impact in rebel-held territory, where many of the nation's hungry and homeless live.

Instead many nongovernmental relief organizations have become active in Sudan. Most of these groups help those hurt by the conflict and do not try to mediate. The International Committee of the Red Cross, for example, has been trying to supply food and medicine to Sudan's hard-pressed population throughout the civil war. Red Cross aid workers have often paid a price for their efforts. A pro-government rebel in southern Sudan named Kerubino Kwanyin Bol kidnapped three Red Cross workers in 1995. He released them only after then-U.S. Congressman Bill Richardson (who in 1997 became U.S. ambassador to the United Nations) ransomed the trio with promises of a large supply of food and equipment. At other times, both rebel and government forces have shot at Red Cross aid flights or stolen aid before it could reach the people who need it. The government has also entirely banned the Red Cross from a few areas where their help could save thousands of lives.

Similar experiences have befallen other aid agencies—from the UN's World Food Program to various religious organizations. Many Christian groups, because they have congregations in Sudan,

In December 1996, former U.S. congressman Bill Richardson (seated second from right) *met with Kerubino Kwanyin Bol* (center) *to negotiate the release of two captured pilots and a nurse who worked for the Red Cross.*

have tried to help the hungry and the homeless. The New Sudan Council of Churches coordinates efforts among five major Christian denominations—Roman Catholic, Presbyterian, Anglican, Sudan Interior Church, and African Inland Church.

Each of the major denominations also typically operates its own relief efforts. Delivering aid is perhaps easier for these churches than it is for other organizations because their parishes function as staging points for relief efforts. Nevertheless, some of these Christian groups have complained that the Sudanese government's Relief and Development Agency has not only slighted the non-Muslim populations but has harassed Christian groups trying to aid those bypassed by official help.

Christian Solidarity International (CSI) representative John Eibner pays an Arab trader who calls himself Ahmed el-Noor Bashir about US$13,200 for the freedom of 132 slaves, who are watching the transaction. Some aid groups have criticized CSI's practice of purchasing slaves. These groups argue that even though CSI buys slaves to grant them their freedom, CSI is endorsing the slave trade by participating in it at all.

Worldwide, several nonde-nominational Christian groups have shown an interest in Sudan's plight. One of these is Christian Solidarity International (CSI), first founded in Switzerland but these days with offices in about 20 countries. It delivers aid, tries to rescue people from religious persecution, and is a respected source of inside information about Sudan. It has become prominent in gathering information about the modern slave trade in the country and in orchestrating a movement to buy freedom for slaves. In early 1998, CSI negotiated the release of 132 Sudanese captives.

An organization called Inter Africa Group monitors human-rights abuses and works with other aid organizations to deliver food and services. In 1995 Inter Africa Group was instrumental in delivering food and medical supplies to people in the Nuba Mountains, an area that the Sudanese govern-

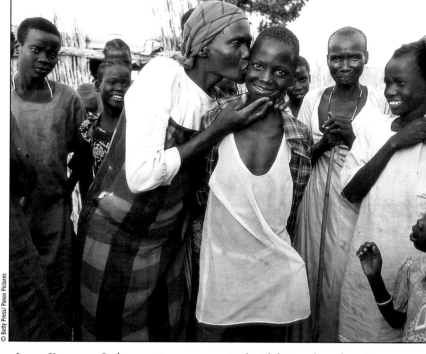

© Betty Press/ Panos Pictures

James Kasara, a Sudanese minor, was reunited with his mother after six years apart. Sudan's civil war has split apart many families. Slave raiders kidnap children and take them north to sell them as slaves. Government and rebel troops force children to join their respective armies.

ment had closed off to aid organizations and other outsiders for 10 years. When Inter Africa Group landed, they encountered many Sudanese who had not seen an aspirin in seven or eight years. Several had been wearing the same clothes for close to a decade, and others were too

ashamed to greet the group because they had no clothes at all. As a result of the organization's efforts, those living in the Nuba Mountains receive regular shipments of food and supplies.

In the same region, Inter Africa Group has worked with Nuba Mountains Solidarity Abroad—an organization that helped citizens build a local democracy—to develop a judicial system. The groups organized a conference in which residents decided what type of

> *When Inter Africa Group landed, they encountered many Sudanese who had not seen an aspirin in seven or eight years.*

> *Sudanese living in a closed area cannot cross government lines. If they do, they are subject to arrest, rape, or execution.*

judicial system they wanted and assisted in the training of judges and police officers.

The refugee problem in Sudan, dealt with mostly by the UNHCR, involves many kinds of refugees. Some are from other countries and have fled to Sudan. Others are Sudanese from one part of the country who have been displaced to a different part. Still others are Sudanese who have left Sudan for other countries. The UNHCR oversees about 30 aid centers and settlement zones within Sudan's borders, where they help the Ethiopians, Eritreans, and other foreign refugees within Sudan. In general, the UNHCR has less to do with Sudanese who have been displaced within Sudan. These refugees gather in shantytowns outside the main cities or simply blend in with local populations wherever they resettle. The Sudanese who have fled to other countries are often aided by UNHCR operations in Uganda, Ethiopia, or other neighboring nations.

INDIVIDUALS

Individual efforts to resolve Sudan's problems are rare, largely because in Sudan there are so many restrictions on what a person can legally say or do. A large in-

The Nuba Mountains, located north of Bahr al-Ghazal in central Sudan, should have been eligible for aid from the government's Relief and Development Agency. Instead, the region was closed to all outsiders, including aid workers, for 10 years.

© D. Moszynski/The Hutchison Library

Um Balaa, located in Darfur province, is one of the many refugee camps found throughout Sudan. The camps house Sudanese escaping from war-torn parts of the country and refugees from neighboring countries such as Ethiopia and Eritrea.

© Caroline Penn / Panos Pictures

ternational aid organization or a church may not have an easy time working in Sudan, but at least it has the strength of numbers and a foreign address to retreat to. A lone woman or man in Sudan speaking out for peace or justice is likely to land in jail or be disposed of by a government or rebel militia. The NIF-led government maintains strict controls on public speech, the press, and any political activity. In such an atmosphere, brave individual action is unlikely.

When private persons have spoken out for peace and justice, it is usually done from the safety of some other country. For example, Dr. Richard Rodgers, an Anglican clergyman from Britain, has made the improvement of Sudan's lot his personal crusade. He camped outside Britain's Foreign Office for 40 days in 1996, consuming only bread and water, to urge the British government to work harder for peace in Sudan. His efforts bore little fruit. Many Sudanese students or professionals living overseas also maintain websites and invite correspondence about the situation in their troubled homeland.

In the United States, a fifth grade class from the Denver, Colorado, area is doing its part to alleviate the slave trade in Sudan. When teacher Barbara Vogel

In the village of Leer, construction workers build a new school close to where an old school—a war casualty—once stood.

brought a newspaper article about a 13-year-old Dinka girl who had recently been freed from slavery into class, her students were shocked. They began to save money to buy the freedom of more slaves.

NO END IN SIGHT

It seems that the worse the problem becomes, the harder the Sudanese and their foreign sympathizers work to solve it. Reluctant Islamists in the government may be forced to yield under popular unrest just to keep the nation alive. Food riots in the Three Towns have brought down governments before and may do so again. Or uncompromising rebels may find themselves unable to hold a countryside where people are sick of war, tired of forced service in militias, and angry about their burned-out crops and stolen children.

The Sudanese know their standard of living is among the world's lowest. The Sudanese may sense this even more strongly as other areas of east central Africa emerge from war and dictatorship and begin to enjoy renewed productivity. The divisive issues that nourish perpetual war in Sudan—sharia against secularism, one tariqa against another, southern separatists against integrationists—may not seem worth the sacrifice. The prospect of a better life from a war-free oil industry, better water distribution, and an infrastructure that is not half a century out-of-date may eventually prove irresistible. ⊕

Fifth Graders Take Action

The article that caught the attention of Barbara Vogel and her fifth-grade class in Denver, Colorado, appeared in the *Rocky Mountain News* in February 1998. By focusing on the experiences of Akuac Malong, a young Dinka girl who spent more than half of her life in slavery, the article unfolded the story of a thriving slave trade in Sudan.

In the article, Abuong Malong, Akuac's mother, remembered the day her six-year-old daughter was taken. Mother and daughter were drawing water from the community well when Arab militiamen rode on camels and horses into their village of Rumalong.

"I was running with Akuac for the trees when a horseman grabbed her," Abuong explains, "I was afraid that if I chased the horseman, he would kill me."

Akuac and her brother were tied to horsebacks and taken north with others from the village to an area close to the city of Kordofan, where Akuac was sold to an Arab man. As a slave, she was made to wash clothes, fetch water, gather firewood, and help cook the meals. The only food Akuac was given to eat were scraps from the table. She slept in

On a class trip in May 1998, Barbara Vogel's fifth graders shouted "let freedom ring" from a mountaintop in the Colorado Rockies.

the kitchen and states that she was treated very badly. Her master attempted to convert Akuac to Islam by taking her to the mosque. He gave her the Muslim name of Fatima. But the girl prayed and remained true to her Christian beliefs.

A trader named Ahmed el-Noor Bashir purchased Akuac and 130 other slaves and brought them to Madhol, a town located 720 miles southwest of Khartoum. There, the humanitarian group Christian Solidarity International bought the slaves and set them free. For the Malong family, the reunion was bittersweet. Akuac's brother, Makol, had been killed two years earlier while trying to escape from his master. Akuac's mother cried when she saw her daughter for the first time in seven years, although she recognizes her daughter only by her teeth. "She was very small when she was taken, her features have changed, but she came back in spirit."

EPILOGUE*

By the end of 1998, little change had come to Sudan. If anything, conditions in the southern provinces had gotten worse. In Bahr al-Ghazal, as many as 700,000 people risked starvation. When the government in Khartoum finally lifted bans on relief flights into the south in late April, Operation Lifeline did not have enough chartered planes to deliver the necessary supplies and food. On July 15, the SPLA announced a three-month cease-fire in Bahr al-Ghazal province to allow the delivery of relief supplies. The government agreed to a one-month truce in the same area.

Elsewhere the civil war raged on. Reports from Khartoum indicated that, beginning on September 14, the government troops engaged in heavy fighting with SPLA rebels and Ugandan and Eritrean troops in the southern province of Eastern Equatoria. In early October, the government announced a general military mobilization against what it claimed was aggressive action by Eritrea and Uganda. Eritrea and Uganda both denied that their troops had entered Sudan or that they had anything to do with the SPLA. Most of the fighting centered around Torit, a town near Juba and a key military gain for the SPLA as the group tried to seize Juba.

Renewed fighting has endangered the lives of 52,000 Sudanese living near Juba. Beginning on September 20, more than 800 people left Juba and 1,800 fled from Torit. Aid workers in the area worried that the fighting would threaten the Bahr al-Ghazal cease-fire (which was scheduled to expire on October 15) and derail deliveries of food and supplies. Meanwhile, the government threw aid workers for another loop on October 1, when it imposed a blanket ban on aid flights delivering supplies to the south. Aid workers feared that the new ban was a sign of possible escalation in the civil war.

Hopes for an end to the famine hinge on peace. On October 7, the Inter-Governmental Authority on Development was scheduled to assist in negotiations between the Khartoum government and the SPLA to lengthen the cease-fire and to possibly extend the area covered by it.

*Please note: The information presented in *Sudan: North against South* was current at the time of the book's publication. For the most recent information about the conflict, look for articles in the international section of U.S. daily newspapers. *The Economist*, a weekly magazine, is also a good source for up-to-date information. You may wish to access, via the Internet, The Latest News from Sudan At Sudan Net at http://www.sudan.net/wwwboard/news. For more general information regarding Sudan, access The Sudan Page at http://sudan.net.

CHRONOLOGY

ca. 2000 B.C.   Ancient Nile Valley civilization flourishes in Egypt and northern Sudan (Nubia).

ca. A.D. 632   Military conquests bring Islam to Egypt and northern Sudan.

1315–1500   Islam displaces Christianity in all of the northern kingdoms and city-states of Sudan.

1500s   Dinka and Nuer peoples move into their present-day territories in southern Sudan.

1517   The Ottoman Turks take over Egypt and make it part of the Ottoman Empire.

1810s   Muhammad Ali becomes the Ottoman governor of Egypt. Ali sends his son, Ismail, to conquer scattered sultanates and kingdoms of Sudan, including areas south of the Sudd.

ca. 1820   The Ottoman regime called Turkiya begins. Ottoman Turks extend postal service and telegraph lines to settlements in northern Sudan.

1870s   The Suez Canal opens and the British take an interest in Egypt and Sudan. Turkiya appoints British soldier Charles Gordon as an administrator in Equatoria.

1881   A Sudanese holy man claims to be the Mahdi and calls for Sudanese Muslims to rebel against the Turkiya.

1884   British send General Charles Gordon's troops to Khartoum to repel the Mahdists. But a year later, Gordon is killed and his troops admit defeat.

1898   Under the leadership of General Herbert Horatio Kitchener, British and Egyptian troops finally defeat the Mahdists.

1899   The British and the Egyptians establish a system of joint control over Sudan, called the Anglo-Egyptian Condominium.

1906   The British, who have worked to develop northern infrastructure, open Port Sudan. At the same time, Christian missionaries set up and operate medical clinics and schools in the south.

1922   Britain approves Egypt's independence. Sudan remains under British control.

1923–24   When British and Egyptian talks over the fate of Sudan fail, nationalist groups riot. Sir Lee Stack, Sudan's governor-general, is assassinated in Cairo. The British respond by enacting the Closed Districts Ordinance, which declares southern Sudan off limits to outsiders.

1948   British gradually move toward an independent Sudan by setting up the Advisory Council for Northern Sudan and establishing a legislative assembly.

1953   Elections produced a parliament, led by the NUP, that begins operating in 1954.

1955   On August 18 southern soldiers of a Juba-based army unit mutiny. Many rebels escape into the woods, where they organize to fight a civil war. On December 19, the Sudanese parliament declares Sudan's independence.

1958   Following three years of factional bickering and antigovernment demonstrations, General Ibrahim Abboud, in conjunction with the Umma Party, stages the first of Sudan's military coups.

1962   The government outlaws expressions of religious and cultural differences in the south.

1963   Anya Nya, the most prominent group of southern military resistance organizations, forms.

1964   In October northern students lead a general uprising to protest the government's lack of action on economic and educational reform. Opposition eventually forces Abboud to resign.

1965   Legislative elections are held. Under the direction of Muhammed Ahmad Mahjub, the Umma party leads a coalition. Mahjub's government sends troops into southern Sudan. By the late 1960s, the fighting has killed about 500,000 Sudanese.

1969   Colonel Jaafar al-Nimeiri stages a military coup.

1972   In February the SSLM and the Nimeiri government sign the Addis Ababa (Peace) Agreement. For the next few years, Nimeiri pushes forward with development projects.

1973–74   Several groups try to overthrow the government. Nimeiri responds by jailing dissidents and declaring a state of emergency.

1977   Nimeiri appoints Hassan al Turabi to the important government post of attorney general.

1983   Nimeiri reforms Sudanese law according to sharia. Full-scale civil war erupts in the south. John Garang forms the SPLA and the SPLM.

1985   General Abdul Rahman Suar el-Dahab overthrows Nimeiri and takes control of Sudan. More than two million Sudanese face starvation due to drought and famine.

1986   UP wins April elections and Sadiq al-Mahdi becomes the prime minister for the second time.

1988   Famine conditions worsen when severe floods destroy Sudanese crops. In March the UN enacts an emergency plan called Operation Lifeline. Although aid workers plan to deliver 100,000 tons of food and supplies, shipments rot in railway cars after the government bans traffic to the south.

1989   In July Brigadier General Omar Hassan Ahmad al-Bashir seizes power.

1991   SPLA splits. Riek Machar becomes head of the Southern Sudan Defense Force (SSDF). The SSDF begins working with al-Bashir's government to counter Garang's troops.

1994   IGAD arranges for the Sudanese government and the southern rebel leaders to meet. Peace talks fail when al-Bashir's government rejects the agreement and both sides refuse to budge.

1996   The government holds elections to bring new members to the National Assembly. The NIF wins most of the seats, Turabi becomes the speaker of the assembly, and al-Bashir is reelected as president. No outside parties were on-hand to ensure that the election was fair.

1997   On April 21, representatives of the NIF and the SSIM sign a peace agreement, but Garang rejects it. The SPLA joins forces with the National Democratic Alliance (NDA) to fight al-Bashir's regime.

1998   In January NDA and SPLA fighters gain territory near the Ethiopian and Eritrean borders. The government lifts bans on aid flights in February, but still requires that flights be cleared with Khartoum at least one month in advance. In southern Sudan about 700,000 people are in danger of starving. On July 15, government and rebel troops agree to a cease-fire to allow aid workers to deliver food to those in need.

SELECTED BIBLIOGRAPHY

Burr, J. Millard and Robert O. Collins. *Requiem for the Sudan: War, Drought, and Disaster Relief on the Nile.* Bolder, CO: Westview Press, 1995.

Daly, M.W. and Ahmad Alawas Sikainga. *Civil War in the Sudan.* New York: St. Martin's Press, 1993.

Deng, Francis M. *War of Visions: Conflict of Identities in the Sudan.* Washington, D.C.: The Brookings Institution, 1995.

Metz, Helen Chapin. *Sudan: A Country Study.* Washington: Federal Research Division, Library of Congress, 1991.

"Militant Ousted, Sudan Asserts." *International Herald Tribune.* June 6, 1996.

Moss, Joyce and George Wilson. *Africans South of the Sahara.* Detroit, MI: Gale Research, Inc., 1991.

Pettit, Barbara. Report of rebel action in Wau and near Kassala. BBC World Service. February 7, 1998.

"Sudanese Rebels Claim to Capture Army Posts." *International Herald Tribune.* January 15, 1997.

Weiner, Tim. "The Grand Vizier of Islam, or Chief Terrorist?" *International Herald Tribune.* December 26, 1996.

INDEX

ABOUT THE AUTHOR

Lawrence J. Zwier is a writer, editor, and university lecturer who has lived and worked in Minnesota, Saudi Arabia, Malaysia, and Japan. He lives in Singapore with his wife and two children.

ABOUT THE CONSULTANT

Andrew Bell-Fialkoff, *World in Conflict* series consultant, is a specialist on nationalism, ethnicity, and ethnic conflict. He is the author of *Ethnic Cleansing*, published by St. Martin's Press in 1996, and has written numerous articles for *Foreign Affairs* and other journals. He is writing a book on the role of migration in the history of the Eurasian steppe. Bell-Fialkoff lives in Bradford, Massachusetts.